# Success Skills

## for High School, College, and Career

Cary J. Green, PhD

*Cary J Green*

First published by Dog Ear Publishing
4011 Vincennes Rd
Indianapolis, IN 46268
www.dogearpublishing.net

ISBN: 978-1-4575-5814-6

This book is printed on acid-free paper.

Printed in the United States of America

# Contents

# Testimonials for
*Success Skills for High School, College, and Career*

"This unique and inspirational book teaches students how to be successful in school right now, while developing the skills that employers absolutely need in the 21st century. Just the soft skills discussion alone, including critical thinking and problem-solving, working with others, professional communication, and time management, makes this a one of a kind resource that every student must have and use to empower their future. I also highly recommend this book for parents and teachers who want to build success skills in their students."

—Pat Wyman, "America's Most Trusted Learning Expert" and CEO of HowToLearn.com.

"*Believing* you can achieve success is fundamental to *achieving* success. Cary Green's excellent new book can help you understand your skills and abilities so that you have the confidence to go for it—confidence to take action—actions that put you on the path to a thriving, successful life. Don't limit your future based on your current skills. Empower your future by learning from Cary and his wonderful book."

—Rebecca Kochenderfer, CEO of Homeschool.com.

"What does it take to prepare students to be college and career ready? The roadmap to get there can be found by nailing down these essential soft skills outlined in this book. Training is an investment worth making for a long-term, strategic path for your career. A proper understanding of your level of soft skills self-awareness is a major step in assessing motives and values for creating collaborative teams. The attributes, traits, and characteristics that Cary Green has defined in his *Success Skills* will serve you well in becoming an influential leader. Beyond advancing your college and career goals, these soft skills can make your life richer and more meaningful."

—Audrey Halpern, soft-skills trainer at ARH Training.

"*Success Skills* contains a simple, yet powerful set of keys that will unlock the doors standing between you and all you can be - all you are meant to be; no matter your circumstances. That's a crucial distinction, too. No matter your past, no matter your present difficulties or obstacles. Dr. Green's easy to grasp book is a road map bursting with science-backed information, tips and advice in a clear, step-by-step plan, as well as a psychological primer illuminating the missing link between self-doubt and self-awareness; leading you to the gateway of self-confidence and achievement."

—R.A. Conroy, Award-winning filmmaker and author
of *Shelter – Lost and Found.*

# Acknowledgments

I thank the many high school and college students, high school teachers, university professors, career counselors, advisors, parents, soft-skills trainers, and early career professionals who provided helpful feedback. Your efforts greatly improved this book.

I also want to thank the staff at Dog Ear Publishing for their efforts in making this book a reality.

# Preface

This book is the second edition of *Leadership and Soft Skills for Students: Empowered to Succeed in High School, College, and Beyond*. This new edition maintains the themes that intelligence is not enough and that skills enable you to perform at the level of your ability.

Although many of the leadership and soft skills included in the original book contribute to academic success, two new chapters specifically focused on academic success skills are included in this edition. The broader title of this edition reflects the inclusion of academic success skills.

This edition contains an expanded discussion of critical thinking and professional communication. Data are provided to demonstrate the importance of success skills. The "Overview of the Three Rs" has been restructured. The final chapter has been revised to provide perspective and guidance for putting into practice the advice provided in the book. Several other enhancements have been made based on discussion with end users.

Thank you for your interest in *Success Skills for High School, College, and Career.*

# Dedication

To Nell and Reshma.

# Introduction

Do you want to enhance your academic performance now and prepare for future career success? Do you want to grow as a leader? If so, you must build a skill set that enables you to perform at the level of your ability.

For example, consider two students who have the same academic ability. One student attends class regularly and takes detailed notes. He participates in study groups and excels at preparing for and taking tests. This student, who demonstrates academic success skills, will perform at a higher level than the student who lacks academic success skills.

I know this example is accurate because I was the student who lacked academic success skills. I graduated in the top 10% of my high school class, but earned a D during my first semester in college. (Frankly, I was surprised that my grade turned out that high.) That experience motivated me to develop my academic success skills.

During my twenty years as a university professor, I taught many students who took their performance to the next level by developing their academic success skills. Unfortunately, I taught many others whose performance was limited by a lack of these important skills.

Further, my interaction with employers confirmed that graduates who demonstrate leadership and soft skills stand out from their peers. I wrote this book to help you understand and build skills essential for academic success and career readiness. The skills are practical, impactful, and immediately applicable. Specifically, you will:

1.  construct realistic expectations for achieving success,

2. develop self-awareness,

3. build a future-oriented attitude, and

4. improve your academic success skills, leadership skills, and soft skills.

We will discuss key concepts of achieving success, and you will construct realistic expectations for achieving success. You will understand that intelligence alone won't make you successful and that developing your skills enables you to perform at the level of your ability. You will discover the need to develop new skills each time you advance in your education and career. And you will learn that many successful people stumble a time or two on the journey to success; if you don't understand this fact, you may mistakenly believe that a setback can prevent you from achieving success.

Successful people are reflective and understand themselves, and you, too, will develop self-awareness. You will learn to utilize your strengths and manage your weaknesses. Developing your self-awareness ensures that you understand your values and motives, and this understanding will empower you to engage in the right activities for the right reasons.

Successful people engage in activities today that benefit their future, and you will build a future-oriented attitude. You will learn to seek and engage in opportunities that enhance your success skills; many of these opportunities are discussed in this book.

Ultimately, you will improve your academic success skills, leadership skills, and soft skills via our discussion and by completing hands-on exercises. These skills will contribute to your success in school, on the job, and in your relationships.

# Success Skills Defined

Academic success skills are techniques and actions that allow you to perform at the level of your academic ability. Successful students develop effective study skills such as note-taking and reading for understanding. These students think critically and excel at preparing for and taking exams. Successful students utilize resources ranging from teachers and advisors to academic success centers. These students actively engage in their education and participate in learning communities and study groups. They also participate in experiential education opportunities and develop portfolios to showcase their accomplishments.

Leadership often is equated to influence (Maxwell, 2007). Leaders have the influence to move people toward a common goal. The greater your leadership ability, the greater your ability to leverage the skills and abilities of others. Leaders can accomplish more through the people they lead than they can by themselves. You must develop your leadership skills if you want to influence others and truly make a difference in your family, school, community, workplace, and world. You will discover that leadership is not dependent on your title, and you may be in a leadership role now.

I define soft skills as "a collection of abilities, behaviors, and attitudes that increase your effectiveness." Soft skills differ from, but are complementary to, technical (or hard) skills. Successful engineers must certainly possess the knowledge and technical skills of engineering. Successful engineers must also demonstrate soft skills such as communication, critical thinking, and professionalism and be able to work effectively with clients and coworkers.

Soft skills are not tied to any career or discipline and are sometimes called "transferable skills." Students who develop their soft skills can enhance their academic performance and transfer the skills to their future career.

Common examples of soft skills include:

1. Critical thinking and problem-solving

2. Written and oral communication

3. Ability to work effectively on a team

4. Time management

5. Strong work ethic

6. Resiliency

## The Importance of Success Skills

Noted leadership expert John Maxwell states that "leadership ability determines effectiveness" (Maxwell, 2007). In other words, the greater your leadership ability, the greater your potential to influence others and achieve success. Further, a recent survey by the National Association of Colleges and Employers (National Association of Colleges and Employers, 2017) showed that 80 percent of employers look for evidence of leadership skills when evaluating potential employees.

Employers also place a high value on soft skills. Career-Builder surveyed two thousand human resources specialists and found that 77 percent ranked soft skills as important as hard skills (CareerBuilder, 2014). Despite the importance of soft skills, employers commonly report them as lacking in new hires. Adecco Staffing surveyed five hundred senior executives and found that 92 percent reported skills deficits in new hires, and 44 percent reported a lack of soft skills (Adecco Staffing, 2013).

Academic success skills are important for academic performance and timely graduation. According to the US Department of Education (US Department of Education, 2015a), less than 40 percent of students who enroll in a public, four-year institution actually graduate in four years. The percentage increases to about 50 percent after five years and to about 60 percent after six years.

Students who graduate with their "four-year" degree in five or six years do so at great expense. The average annual cost of a public, four-year college in the US is about $18,000 (US Department of Education, 2015b). The average starting salary of a college graduate is about $50,000 (National Association of Colleges and Employers, 2016). Thus, a student who takes an extra year to graduate essentially loses $68,000 ($18,000 in tuition costs and $50,000 in lost income). The amount doubles to a $136,000 loss for students who take an extra two years.

Although many factors influence academic performance, many students can improve their performance and achieve a more timely graduation by utilizing academic success skills.

## Developing Success Skills

I believe there are three keys to developing success skills. First, you must know what you need to know. We will discuss many aspects of achieving success, and you will discover much of what you need to know to be successful. Second, you must put forth the effort necessary to develop the abilities and behaviors that you need.

Maintaining the right attitude is the third key to developing your success skills. Maintaining a positive attitude is vital to your success. Although you may get discouraged or frustrated from time to time, your positive attitude will give you the emotional buoyancy needed to move ahead. Successful leaders control their attitude even when they cannot control their circumstances.

Further, successful leaders recognize their potential, demonstrate confidence, and truly believe they can succeed. Please understand that believing you can succeed does not mean that you are arrogant or think you are better than others. Rather, belief in yourself provides the confidence needed to step up to challenges and to handle setbacks.

Successful leaders balance their confidence with humility. Genuine humility indicates inner strength and security. Humility allows leaders to admit when they are wrong, to seek input from others, and to respond appropriately to constructive criticism. Humble leaders gladly share credit and are quick to praise others.

You will grow as a person and as a leader as you put forth effort to learn and apply the concepts in this book. Don't let a lack of confidence hold you back. I know several successful people who have overcome setbacks or who were told they would not succeed. As I mentioned above, I nearly dropped out of college because of poor academic performance.

Finally, I challenge you to never give up on your journey to success. Sheer determination and "want to" are powerful tools that will help you succeed. You can accomplish much in life if you dare to believe in yourself, make the commitment to succeed, and put forth real effort.

# Getting the Most Out of This Book

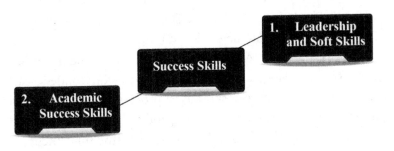

You will discover leadership and soft skills within a framework of "readiness," "relationships," and "results." Readiness teaches you self-awareness and emphasizes the need to understand yourself, maintain a positive attitude, look for and take advantage of opportunities, and overcome challenges. Relationships teaches you to communicate effectively, forge authentic connections in your personal and professional life, and be professional. Results teaches you to be future-oriented and emphasizes the need to know your values and priorities, set and achieve goals, solve problems, and be accountable. Readiness focuses on you. Relationships focuses on your interactions with others. Results focuses on your ability to get the job done.

Many leadership and soft skills contribute to academic success, so you will learn them first. You will then learn specific academic success skills. You will develop your academic success skills by utilizing academic best-practices and by using academic success resources.

I suggest you read this book in its entirety to get the big picture *before* you answer the questions or work the exercises.

As you read, keep a journal of the thoughts and questions that come to mind. Once you have read the whole book, read it again, answering the questions and working the exercises within each chapter. Review the summary at the end of each chapter. Review again material that is not clear.

Seek a mentor to hold you accountable and help you on your journey. Make a commitment to grow and understand that developing success skills is a process. If you want to improve your three-point shooting ability, you can't just read a book on basketball— you first must learn the fundamentals of shooting and then shoot a lot of three-pointers. Developing your success skills is similar—you must understand success skills and then purposefully work to develop those skills.

Finally, please reflect on what you learn in each chapter by answering the following questions:

1.  In your own words, explain the main points of the chapter.

2.  What are the three most significant things you learned from the chapter?

3.  List three specific actions you will take to apply what you learned in the chapter.

4.  What benefit will you experience by following through on these actions?

# References

Adecco Staffing. September 30, 2013. *Lack of Soft Skills Negatively Impacts Today's U.S. Workforce.* Retrieved May 22, 2017 from Adecco Staffing: http://www.adeccousa.com/about/press/Pages/20130930-lack-of-soft-skills-negatively-impacts-todays-us-workforce.aspx.

CareerBuilder. April 10, 2014. "Overwhelming Majority of Companies Say Soft Skills Are Just as Important as Hard Skills." Retrieved September 12, 2017 from CareerBuilder.com: http://www.careerbuilder.com/share/aboutus/pressreleasesdetail.aspx?sd=4%2f10%2f2014&siteid=cbpr&sc_cmp1=cb_pr817_&id=pr817&ed=12%2f31%2f2014

Maxwell, J. 2007. *The 21 Irrefutable Laws of Leadership.* Nashville: Thomas Nelson.

National Association of Colleges and Employers. November 16, 2016. "Salary Survey: The Early Drivers of Class of 2016 Gains." Retrieved May 22, 2017 from Naceweb.org: http:// www.naceweb.org/job-market/compensation/salary-survey- the-early-drivers-of-class-of-2016-gains/.

National Association of Colleges and Employers. April 3, 2017. "Job Outlook 2016: The Attributes Employers Want to See on New College Graduates' Resumes." Retrieved May 22, 2017 from Naceweb.org: http:// www.naceweb.org/ career-development/trends-and-predictions/job-outlook-2016-attributes-employers-want-to-see-on-new-college-graduates-resumes/.

US Department of Education, National Center for Education Statistics. 2015a. Integrated Postsecondary Education Data System (IPEDS), Fall 2002 and Spring 2007 through Spring 2015, Graduation Rates component. (Table 326.10. December 2015.)

US Department of Education, National Center for Education Statistics. 2015b. Integrated Postsecondary Education Data System (IPEDS), Fall 2000 through Fall 2014, Institutional Characteristics component. (Table 330.10. December 2015.)

# Part I: Readiness

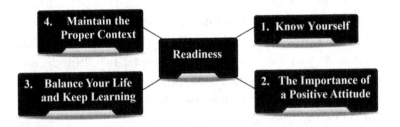

In this book, I discuss readiness in terms of being prepared to handle whatever comes your way. Successful people are ready to take advantage of opportunities and to handle occasional setbacks. My expectation is that you will be ready and that you will continue to grow as a leader and ultimately achieve great success in your life. To be ready, you must know yourself, maintain a positive attitude, balance your life, keep learning, and maintain the proper context.

Knowing yourself means that you are self-aware and know your strengths and weaknesses. Each of us has unique strengths, and you are more effective when utilizing your strengths. Similarly, managing your weaknesses is critical for your success. When you evaluate your weaknesses, you may find that an apparent weakness can often be overcome by working harder and smarter.

Challenging yourself requires you to step up to activities or responsibilities that stretch you. Doing so refines your existing skills and builds new skills. The new-and-improved skills will bolster your confidence and provide momentum for further growth. Reflecting on your experiences will help you grow even more. Experience is a great teacher—if you reflect and learn from your experiences. Reflecting on things that stress you and motivate you can help you identify the need to take a break or change directions.

Attitude is a critically important component of readiness. Your attitude has a great influence on your relationships, productivity, and happiness. If you want to be a successful leader, then learn to maintain a positive attitude; this attitude will inspire and encourage the people around you. Furthermore, a positive attitude will help you overcome setbacks and struggles you will encounter. A negative attitude, however, can damage your relationships and undermine your skills. Surrounding yourself with positive people helps you maintain a positive attitude.

Readiness requires that you balance your life and never stop learning. If your life is out of balance, long-term success and happiness will be difficult to achieve. Balance is achieved when you spend quality time in each of the important areas of your life. Furthermore, look for opportunities to learn throughout your life. Consider that graduation ceremonies are called "commencement" ceremonies because your education is just beginning.

Readiness requires that you maintain the proper context so you don't get so caught up in what you are doing that you lose sight of your overall goal. If you lose sight, you can burn out and want to give up. Keep focused on your big goals while working on small, and occasionally boring, steps along the way to your goal. Maintaining the proper context also can help you stay motivated after a loss or setback. Don't lose sight of the big picture of your life if you fail occasionally or struggle. Don't focus on what knocked you down; focus on what you can achieve.

Although being ready makes sense, sometimes we can be tempted to "wing it," rather than working hard to prepare. If you are not prepared, you may not fail, but you likely won't perform at a high level. As will be discussed later, successful people consistently perform at a high level, and their productivity is not limited by a lack of effort.

You may have been successful in the past without need for much preparation. As you progress through life, however, going in unprepared will not always work. Adopting a sports analogy, teams may win a few games when unprepared but certainly will lose many more—especially as the competition get tougher.

The bottom line is that you must be ready to take advantage of opportunities, to overcome challenges, and to reach your goals. Developing your success skills will enhance your readiness.

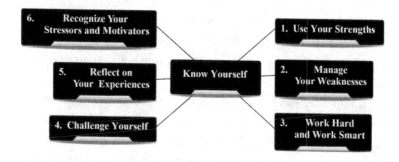

# Chapter 1: Know Yourself

Knowing yourself enables you to take advantage of opportunities and overcome challenges. We each have skills, abilities, and perspectives that allow us to make unique contributions. The better you recognize your strengths and your unique ability to make a difference, the readier you will be to leverage your opportunities.

Your strengths will help you only if you use them. A colleague of mine has a program he calls "The I in Team." You probably have heard that there is no "I" in team. My colleague, however, teaches that each individual team member must contribute to the overall success of the team. Don't misinterpret this "I" as being the star of the team, but use your strengths so your team succeeds. By making strong contributions to a successful team, you set yourself up for opportunities as an individual.

## Use Your Strengths

Successful people use their strengths. Of course, you must identify your strengths before you can use them. The following questions will give you insight into your strengths:

1. What do you think your strengths are?

2. What do your friends tell you that your strengths are? (Ask three or four friends.)

3. What are you passionate about?

4. What do people ask you to do?

You likely have strengths that are not developed fully, and you likely have strengths that have not been identified by the questions above. You can find additional resources online. If you are a student, contact your advisor or counselor to identify resources. University students can find resources at the campus career center. Additionally, ask your mentor what he sees as your strengths.

Please list your strengths below:

1.

2.

3.

4.

5.

Once you know your strengths, leverage them. For example, if you have strength in communication, write for your school's newspaper, start a blog, or enter a public-speaking competition.

Creating opportunities to use your strengths allows your strengths to create opportunities for you. Writing a blog for your school gives you networking visibility that can lead to other opportunities. Plus, your blogging experience enhances your resume and can pay dividends when you apply for college, scholarships, awards, and jobs.

Below, list opportunities to leverage your strengths, and then make a commitment to follow through on each opportunity.

1.

2.

3.

4.

5.

## Manage Your Weaknesses

Successful people manage their weaknesses and leverage their strengths. Nearly everyone has areas that can be improved. It takes courage to admit weaknesses, and it takes discipline to change. Success requires a commitment to making necessary changes.

To begin identifying your weaknesses, answer the following questions:

1. What do you think your weaknesses are?

2. What do your friends tell you that your weaknesses are? (Ask three or four friends.)

3. What do you try to avoid doing? (We often avoid areas of weakness.)

4. What has caused you to fail to complete a task or perform at a high level?

5. What has caused problems in your relationships?

Use the information derived from the questions, and then list your areas for improvement:

1.

2.

3.

4.

5.

The following are some steps to help you manage your weaknesses:

1. Identify your weakness.

2. Believe you can improve.

3. Find resources.

4. Create a plan to manage your weakness.

5. Define its impact.

6. Implement your plan.

7. Assess your progress.

8. Celebrate your progress.

Identifying your weakness is the first step in managing that weakness. For example, if you often fail to complete assignments, get your work done late, or often rush through and fail to produce quality work, then you likely have a weakness in time management.

The second step is believing you can improve the weakness. Third, find resources such books, online videos, or an in-person seminar, then learn how others have managed the same weakness. Your mentor can be an excellent resource.

Fourth, use your resources to create a plan to manage your weakness. Be sure to define the impact (step five) by answering this question: How will improving the weakness benefit me? To stay motivated, regularly refer to your impact statement.

Sixth, implement your plan, and then periodically assess your progress (step seven). Even small improvements are good and show that you are making progress. Finally, celebrate your progress (step eight), and don't be discouraged if the process takes a while.

Here's an example of how I used the steps outlined above to overcome one of my weaknesses. I identified perfectionism by reflecting on the fact that I had several projects that were "almost" finished. I knew I could finish the projects—*if* I could get over my need for perfection. I asked my mentor for advice. She asked if I brushed my teeth all day, and I told her that I did not. She said, "Of course you don't. You decide when you have done your best, and then you move on." She encouraged me to use the same philosophy on my projects. I must decide when I have done enough work to satisfy the goal of the project, and then stop putting in additional time that ultimately does little to improve the project.

I took her advice and finished several projects, which freed up time for other things. My outcomes were that I was getting more work done, and I was maintaining the quality of my work. I still must deliberately guard against perfectionism, but I am making great progress. You, too, can make progress if you follow the steps listed above.

As you identify your weaknesses, recognize that some may be overexpressed strengths. My weakness of perfectionism is rooted in my strength of striving to produce quality outcomes. My competitiveness also can be overexpressed to the point that I sometimes focus on results and not on people. This tendency is a weakness in relationships. Reflect on your weaknesses to identify when you are diminishing your effectiveness by doing too much of a good thing.

You also can manage your weaknesses by letting someone cover for you. For example, assume you are an officer for a club at your school. Your club must plan an event and present the plan to teachers and fellow students. If you are a great planner but have a weakness in public speaking, help develop the plan and let another officer present it. Work closely with the other officer to develop your communication skills and commit to giving a presentation in the future.

## Work Hard and Work Smart

An apparent weakness in ability may be overcome with hard work and/or by learning new skills. I have seen many young people who felt they had a weakness holding them back or preventing them from overcoming an obstacle discover that the weakness represented the need to work harder and smarter.

Let me share a personal example of overcoming a perceived weakness. As mentioned earlier, I received a D in my first-semester college chemistry course. I assumed my weakness was the inability to succeed in college overall. I thought I would never understand chemistry, and I considered quitting school.

Fortunately, I decided to try again. I repeated the course and earned an A. I worked harder and smarter. I don't think my IQ increased, but I developed my academic success skills, and these skills made me "smarter." Remember that success skills enable you to perform at the level of your ability.

What can we learn from this example? My "weakness" was not my perceived lack of ability. I had the intelligence to get an A, but I had to work harder and smarter to earn the A. Working hard is crucial but is often not enough to overcome apparent weaknesses. If you don't realize this fact, you may work hard but not get the results you want. This situation is quite frustrating and can cause you to quit. To improve my performance in chemistry, I worked smarter by developing and utilizing academic success skills.

Remember that one of your learning outcomes is constructing a realistic expectation of achieving success. This example shows that you must work harder and also develop new skills as you advance in your education. I tried to succeed in college using the same skills and effort I had used in high school. This approach did not work.

I learned another important lesson through this experience: a failure can catalyze future success. The class that I thought would end my college career caused me to reflect on my performance, identify my real limitations, and create a strategy to move forward.

I did not know whether I would ever understand college chemistry, and I easily could have given up. Rather than giving up, however, I tried again, and I succeeded. Looking back, I can see that the trouble I had with chemistry ultimately helped me, but I certainly did not know that at the time. Had I not tried again, I would never have known what I could achieve. I encourage you to never give up, at least not until you have worked harder and smarter.

You undoubtedly will encounter new challenges as you progress into new phases of your life. Once you know yourself and understand your abilities, you will be ready to conquer increasingly difficult challenges. I have heard it said that difficult challenges don't bother us nearly as much as *unexpected* difficult challenges. Don't be surprised by difficult challenges in life, but develop the attitude to work harder and smarter until you overcome the challenges.

What if you are working harder and smarter but still struggle? Struggling despite your best effort illustrates the importance of knowing your strengths. An area of interest or activity may not align with an area of strength.

As an example, in my career I have taught and mentored many students who wanted to go to veterinary school. The admission requirements for veterinary schools, however, are quite high. Thus, the stark reality is that some students who intensely want to get into a veterinary school lack the grades to get admitted. Although very disappointing, this reality requires students to change their plans and seek another career. Initially, many students see this change as a failure. This change, however, is *not* a failure. Rather, it demonstrates the need to align effort with an area of strength. I have seen several students go on to have successful careers in other fields.

Remember, we each have strengths and abilities in *some* areas, but not in *all* areas. If you find yourself struggling despite your very best effort, take the time to truly discover your strengths, and then align your efforts with your strengths.

Doing so often requires a change, but ultimately, you will experience greater success—and your frustration will decrease.

If you are a student, align your academic major and career goals with your strengths. To help you evaluate your options, talk to your mentor, teachers, and advisors. You also can take career assessments to help you identify career options that align with your strengths. Many of these assessments are available online and through most university career centers. (More information is provided in the section "Academic Success Resources.")

## Challenge Yourself

Let's switch gears and talk about the importance of challenging yourself. It's easy to avoid activities that are new and different. But doing so prevents you from knowing what you are truly capable of achieving. When you step up to a new challenge, you often learn that your current skills are insufficient for success (as was the case with my academic success skills when I stepped up to college chemistry).

Engaging in challenging situations will catalyze refinement of your existing skills and lead to the development of new skills. New challenges also will allow you to discover abilities that you did not know you had. Therefore, challenging yourself can increase your confidence. As you gain confidence and develop a can-do attitude, you will seek and conquer new challenges, and this cycle will allow you to make continual progress.

Let me share an example in which I challenged myself. When I was a college student working on my bachelor's degree, I took a course designed for students who were working on master's and PhD degrees. I considered dropping the course when I discovered that all my classmates were more academically advanced. I decided to stay in the course, however, and challenge myself. Overall, I did quite well, and I gained skills and perspectives that still benefit me.

That graduate course was intimidating at first, but it ultimately gave me the confidence to go to graduate school. Had I not challenged myself, I would have missed a great opportunity for professional growth. I encourage you to live your life so that you achieve all you can. To do so, you must challenge yourself. Some examples for students include taking a leadership role in an organization in your school or community, or entering a public-speaking competition.

List three challenging activities that could stretch you:

1.

2.

3.

Make a commitment to follow through on each of these activities. Share this list with a friend or a mentor to keep you accountable.

You may be a little nervous when you step up to a new challenge, but nervousness is normal. You may struggle, but struggling is normal. You may make some mistakes, but mistakes are opportunities to learn. Strive to learn something from each of your mistakes, and your mistakes will catalyze your progress.

After you complete your "stretching" activities, answer the following questions:

1. What were you most worried about with this activity?

2. How did you expect the activity to improve your skills?

3. What was the most difficult aspect of this activity?

4. What did you learn about yourself as you stepped up to this activity?

5. Describe how this activity helped you grow.

## Reflect on Your Experiences

Let's talk about reflection, a key process in knowing yourself. Reflection is the process of thinking deeply in retrospect to gain insight. Consider the fact that each of your activities has two outcomes. The first outcome is the impact of the activity itself. The second outcome is the experience and knowledge gained, which you can use in the future. Develop the habit of deliberate reflection so that you learn something from everything you do.

Answer the following questions as you reflect on your experiences:

1. What worked well?

2. What did not work well?

3. What would you do differently if you repeated the project?

4. What did you learn that you can apply to your next project?

As you reflect on your activities, keep in mind that identifying things you could have done differently does *not* mean you did it wrong the first time. Rather, understanding how to improve is a sign that you are gaining new experience and knowledge. Maximize the factors that contribute to your success.

Capture your reflections in a journal. Doing so not only benefits you but can also benefit others. For example, if you are an officer in an organization at your school, you can pass your reflection journal to the person who will have your position next year. The information in your journal will help the new officer succeed and will help your organization improve every year.

Reflect on your setbacks and failures, as well as on your successes. Minimize or eliminate factors that cause you to come up short. Look for patterns. For example, you may see the pattern of frequently missed deadlines. Potential solutions include starting earlier, developing and sticking to a timeline, and staying focused on your priorities. If you are not deliberately reflective, you may not see the patterns, and you may continue to make the same mistakes.

## Recognize Your Stressors and Motivators

The ability to recognize your stressors and motivators is another important aspect of knowing yourself. Sometimes, we simply need to take a break. If you are a highly motivated person like me, you know how hard it can be to recognize the need to take a break. I have wasted time and frustrated myself (and others) by pushing on when I needed to take a break. Perhaps you have done so, as well.

A little stress may motivate you and keep you productively engaged in what you need to do. I seem to work especially hard when preparing for meetings or presentations that I am a little anxious about. Too much stress, however, can make you unproductive.

Do you know your signs of stress? My signs of stress are fatigue, irritability, inability to concentrate, impatience, and adopting a condescending tone. When I find myself exhibiting these symptoms, I know it is time to take a break, get some exercise, get some rest, and rejuvenate. As a young leader, learn to be aware of your stress level and take breaks to rejuvenate yourself as needed.

We just discussed the fact that too much stress can make us unproductive. How do we know if we are productive? Perhaps you have heard someone say, "I studied for three hours, but I did not learn anything." Some people evaluate productivity in terms of how much *time* they put into an activity. Successful people, however, focus on the *results*, rather than the time spent on the task.

In other words, a student should gauge her productivity by how well she is learning her class material, rather than how long she studied. Make no mistake about it: You must invest significant time in your priorities to achieve your goals. Spending time on an activity without gaining the outcome you need, however, is unproductive—and frustrating. In the case of studying, if you find yourself spinning your mental wheels without learning much, talk to your teacher or a tutor to get you back on track. If you feel stressed, take a break to rejuvenate yourself.

Let me illustrate the value of taking a break with the example of preparing for my preliminary examinations in graduate school. These examinations are a cornerstone of the PhD program and can be very difficult. Basically, a PhD student gets questioned by five professors for three hours or so.

At best, the exams are humbling; at worst, you flunk out of graduate school because you fail the exams.

The stress associated with these important exams motivated me to work very hard. I studied day and night for weeks: reviewing class notes, reading books, and scouring scientific manuscripts. Soon, burnout, fatigue, and stress increased. And learning *decreased*.

When I found myself in that situation, I would take a break for a few hours, or even for a day or so. I lost some study time by taking a break, but my burnout, fatigue, and stress decreased. And when I resumed studying, my learning increased.

Initially, I did not think I should stop studying; I did not think I could afford to take a break, even though I was fatigued and was not learning much. But I finally realized that I was more focused on the activity of studying (putting time in) than on the outcome of studying (learning).

Here's my point: If you are a little stressed as you work on something and that stress is motivating you to achieve your goal, you can likely keep working. If, however, the stress is making you unduly worried, unproductive, or causing you to lose sleep, take a short break. Talk with your mentor and your teachers if your stress level doesn't diminish.

In addition to knowing their stressors, successful leaders understand their motives and are driven by the appropriate motives. Positive motives—such as helping, encouraging, and mentoring others; serving your community; and solving problems—should drive you. Negative motives—such as pride, greed, and anger—should be avoided.

Further, successful people avoid making comments to make themselves look good at the expense of others. I remember a quote that my high school baseball coach once shared with us: "Class does not build itself up by tearing others down." I have tried to live my life according to this simple statement. Pride sometimes gets in the way, however, and I make comments for the wrong reasons with the wrong motives. Doing so can damage relationships. The fix is quite simple: Know yourself well enough to recognize when your motives are wrong.

Reflecting on the motivation behind your actions can be quite insightful and can ensure that you do the right things for the right reasons. I once managed a national competition for students. A competitor submitted her project online, but the file became corrupted in the upload process, and the judge disqualified the student because he could not open her file. When I learned what had happened (after the deadline for submission), I contacted the judge and asked him to allow the student to resubmit her project.

My motives were good: I was advocating for a student. As I talked to the judge, however, I realized that he would not allow the student to resubmit. We talked quite a bit, and I became angry. Finally, I realized that the discussion was no longer about the student but had become about the fact that the judge was not doing what I wanted him to do.

Clearly, my motives were no longer pure. It hurt my pride (a poor motivator), but I finally dropped it. Basically, my pride was keeping me in the argument. My motive was to win— not for the sake of the student but for my own pride. Today, I monitor my motivations to ensure that I do the right things for the right reasons.

Key points from chapter 1:

1. Know your strengths—and use them.

2. Know your weaknesses—and manage them.

3. Work hard and smart to overcome apparent weaknesses.

4. A weakness may be an overexpressed strength.

5. You have strengths and abilities in some areas but not in all areas.

6. Align your effort with your strengths.

7. Put yourself in situations that stretch you.

8. Reflect on your experiences.

9. Apply what you learn from your experiences.

10. Focus on results, rather than solely on the time spent on the task.

11. Recognize when you're stressed and need to take a break.

12. Be driven by the right motives.

# Chapter 2: The Importance of a Positive Attitude

Your positive attitude will provide the motivation you need to achieve all you can. I once needed a nearly perfect score on the final exam to get an A in one of my college classes. I could have put forth minimal effort and kept my B in the class. I believed, however, that I could get an A if I put forth a massive effort, so I decided to go for it. I was right. A few years later, I received a scholarship for graduate school, and I just barely squeaked by the minimum GPA requirement. The extra effort I had put into that final exam contributed to the A, and the A contributed to the scholarship.

I have enjoyed some success because I have always tried to be the best I could be. You can increase your likelihood of succeeding by maintaining a positive attitude and striving to be and do your best. That's the way successful leaders live their lives.

# Maintain a Positive Attitude

I worked as a flagger on a road construction crew one summer while in college. Motorists constantly yelled at me for stopping them. At first, I became angry. Finally, I simply ignored them and stopped getting angry. Through all that, I learned two very powerful lessons. First, there are enough jerks in this world, so I don't need to be one. Second, I could not stop motorists from yelling at me, but I could stop myself from getting mad.

You can control your attitude even when you can't control your circumstances. Although this is a very true statement, it's an easy one to forget. Perhaps you have said, "He makes me mad." The truth, however, is that no one can *make* you mad unless you allow the person (or circumstance) to do so.

Controlling your attitude requires you to manage your thoughts. Have you ever envisioned yourself flunking a test or convinced yourself that a situation would not turn out well? If so, you understand how thoughts can create unnecessary stress, and you also understand how that stress can smother a positive attitude.

My mentor helped me maintain a positive attitude by showing me how to stop creating unnecessary stress for myself. After listening to me vent a concern, she asked, "What were you worried about this time last year?" I thought for a while and told her I did not remember. She asked, "What about three months ago?" A few things came to mind but not many. She then asked about last week. Again, I had an item or two on my list of historical worries but not many. Then she taught me the lesson: I often spent a lot of time worrying about things, and rarely should I have worried as much as I did. She said that most things that seem so ominous at the time are often not that bad. Later, we often can't remember things that stressed us.

The next time you feel worried, stressed, or anxious, realistically assess your thinking. You might find that you are stressing yourself unnecessarily. The negative scenario you envision may not be real, but the resulting bad attitude and stress can be very real. And that bad attitude may prevent you from performing at your highest level. You should be realistic, of course, but maintaining a positive attitude is easier if you envision success rather than failure.

Addressing unpleasant situations sooner rather than later also helps you maintain your positive attitude. If you are like me, you may tend to put off things that appear to be unpleasant. Once you have decided what to do, however, it's best to simply do it.

I once dreaded having a very unpleasant conversation with someone. I put the conversation off for a week, and doing so gave me a bad attitude for the entire week. I considered putting off the conversation until the following Monday. Rather than having to worry about the conversation all weekend, however, I talked to the person on Friday. The actual conversation was not nearly as bad as I had imagined; I should not have wasted so much time and energy worrying. Further, having the conversation on Friday allowed me to enjoy my weekend. Acting sooner rather than later allows you to stop worrying and frees up your mind for more productive activities.

What if the situation is as bad as you assumed it would be? Addressing the issue sooner rather than later remains a good approach and minimizes the potential for the issue to worsen. (We will discuss this concept further in "Conquer Procrastination.")

A positive attitude is easier to maintain if you don't take yourself too seriously. Things will happen that make you look foolish; life is too short to let these things bother you. When I was looking for my first job, I got an interview for a university faculty position. I received the itinerary for the interview, which would take place immediately after a professional meeting I was to attend. During the meeting, I contacted people with whom I would interview.

One evening, my wife and I went to a restaurant, and in walked one of the people who would interview me. Because he and I had already met (and because I wanted the job), I waved to him. He smiled, waved back, and walked toward me. I smiled, stood up, and reached out to shake hands. Everything was going well until he moved right past me without even noticing I was there. I don't know who he was going to see, but I know it was not me.

So, there I was, standing, smiling, and looking quite silly. As I tried to figure out what had gone wrong, my wife gently encouraged me to sit down. I was a little embarrassed and felt like an idiot at the time, but I can laugh about it now. My point? Things like this are going to happen. Save yourself a lot of stress by not taking yourself too seriously.

Maintaining a sense of humor helps you maintain a positive attitude. As I get older, I see the value of a good sense of humor more and more. A little well-placed humor often greases the skids of life and keep things in perspective. Remember that humor is good, but it is no substitute for substance. People quickly see through a veil of humor if there is no substance in your words and actions. Sprinkled in the appropriate amounts at the appropriate times, humor can be beneficial. (Please note that I am not talking about being snarky or using sarcasm or jokes to demean others. There is no place for this.)

Maintaining a positive attitude requires discipline, but it is worth it. Try it, and see if you notice a difference in your productivity, your relationships, and your overall outlook on life.

As an example of an unexpected benefit of maintaining a positive attitude, I travel frequently, and of course, things don't always go as planned. I recall one flight that was repeatedly delayed and finally cancelled. When I got to the counter to get rebooked, I told the attendant I realized that the cancellation was not her fault and that I appreciated her effort to rebook my flight. She looked a little surprised by my comments. Several other people had yelled at her, but I chose to have a positive attitude.

When she handed me the new ticket, I noticed that my row assignment had only one digit. I asked her if she had intentionally upgraded me to first class. She smiled and said, "Yes."

Your positive attitude is a gift to those around you, and your positive attitude can benefit *you*, as well.

## The Benefits of a Positive Attitude

A positive attitude confers many benefits to leaders. First, if you are a positive person, people will be drawn to you; this appeal is a key characteristic of a true leader. Second, your attitude can influence your productivity; most people are more productive when they have a positive attitude. Plus, a positive attitude helps you handle life's inevitable setbacks. If you ever tried to pull a beach ball underwater, you know that once you let go, the ball immediately races to the surface. Similarly, your positive attitude gives you buoyancy when life tries to pull you under.

A positive attitude allows a leader to inspire others and helps her obtain buy-in. A positive attitude allows a leader to see potential in others and provides motivation to develop her team. And team members often strive to accomplish more when their leader believes in them. A positive attitude allows a leader to see opportunities rather than problems and to find strategies to move past obstacles.

Your positive attitude enhances your relationships. Think of a person you admire and with whom you most like to spend time. List his or her characteristics below. Then do the same for the person with whom you *least* like to spend time.

List the characteristics of the person with whom you most want to spend time:

1.

2.

3.

4.

5.

List the characteristics of the person with whom you least want to spend time:

1.

2.

3.

4.

5.

What did you learn from this exercise? How many of the characteristics are related to attitude? I predict that the person you wanted to spend time with has characteristics reflective of a positive attitude. Indeed, a positive attitude is a key soft skill for young leaders to maintain. Here are a few examples of a positive attitude that I try to maintain:

1. Encouragement

2. Optimism

3. Appreciation

4. Sense of humor

5. Resiliency

List three specific ways in which you will maintain a positive attitude this week:

1.

2.

3.

Reflect below on your observations. What did you notice this week? Make these actions a permanent part of your life.

## The Limiting Effects of a Bad Attitude

Consider a plant growing in a flower pot. The plant should grow if it has plenty of water, fertilizer, and sunshine. The plant won't grow in dry soil, however, even with plenty of fertilizer and sunshine. Similarly, the "dry soil" of a bad attitude will limit your potential for success, even if you are very talented.

Attitudes such as arrogance, selfishness, disrespect, jealousy, and insecurity all damage relationships. An attitude of doubt or fear limits your potential for success by preventing you from moving forward after a mistake or setback.

A negative attitude can influence how you respond to something you read or hear, and can damage your relationships. I once received an e-mail from a member of my staff, and that e-mail made me mad (more accurately, I *chose* to get mad). I went to her office and told her about the many shortcomings of her e-mail. Shortly after I had returned to my office, she came in and said that she could see how I could interpret her e-mail as I had. She further explained that she had not intended it to be negative.

Her message was clear, but I chose a negative interpretation. The learning point here is that I got mad and had a stern, unpleasant conversation with my staff member, which could have been avoided. The solution is simple: Don't create negativity. Assume the best rather than the worst—if you are going to make an assumption.

Below, list five characteristics of a bad attitude that you exhibit. Make a commitment to work through your list until none remain. Ask a few close friends and your mentor for input; they may see attitude characteristics that you don't.

1.

2.

3.

4.

5.

I will end this section with a few words of caution: Don't get caught up in a "that's not fair" attitude. For a long time, I thought many of my experiences were not fair. It was not fair that I had to work on my uncle's farm while my friends went fishing. It was not fair that my chemistry lab partner did not do enough work. It was not fair that someone backed into my car and drove off without leaving a note.

I finally realized I was stressing over things beyond my control. If you struggle in this area, do what I did: Understand that life is sometimes not going to be fair—then move on. If you let yourself believe that life should be fair, you will be disappointed constantly, which fuels a bad attitude. Further, it's pointless (and dumb) to stress over things you cannot change.

## Your Inner Circle

Earlier, I asked you to list the characteristics of people you do and do not like to spend time with. Let's expand that discussion. Your attitude can be greatly influenced by the attitude of your friends. You likely have lots of friends but only a few friends who are close to you. Your inner circle refers to your closest friends and should include only those people who inspire, encourage, and support you.

I have known several young people who were held back by the attitudes and actions of people in their inner circle. Often, these young people felt awkward when they achieved more than their friends, so they sometimes wouldn't achieve what they otherwise could have. And when they did achieve something, their friends made fun of them. I also have known students who have not performed at their highest level because they hung out with friends who did not work hard or who were content with just getting by; they simply developed the bad attitude of their friends.

If you are surrounded by friends like these, don't let them into your inner circle or allow them to negatively influence your attitude. You can still be friends, but I encourage you to find new friends for your inner circle. I realize that finding new friends can be difficult and that you may not want to distance yourself from some of your close friends. Consider the fact, however, that if you surround yourself with people who have no goals or who have a bad attitude, you will soon think and act like they do.

Several years ago, I had a friend who had a very negative attitude. She would often say, "I can never get it right." I tried hard to encourage her and help her improve her attitude. Her attitude never improved, however, and one day, when I was working on a task, I said out loud, "I can never get this right." I am usually a positive person, so the statement surprised me. But the truth is that if you spend a lot of time with people who have a bad attitude, that attitude will negatively impact you.

Completely avoiding negative people may not be possible. I have worked with people who constantly complain, speak negatively about nearly everything, and point out every reason why things will go wrong. I usually feel worse after talking to those people. I worked with them, however, so I could not completely ignore them, but I did not let them into my inner circle.

On the other hand, I have worked with people and have friends who are always positive, inspiring, and encouraging. These people see potential success instead of seeing every reason why something might fail. I look forward to spending time with these people, and I welcome them into my inner circle. I get energized and encouraged when I talk to them.

Do yourself a favor and fill your inner circle with people who lift you up. These people will contribute to your growth. Surround yourself with people who have:

1.   a positive outlook,

2.   goals and ambitions,

3.   a strong work ethic,

4.   an encouraging attitude,

5.   the ability to inspire you to achieve, and

6.   the self-confidence to celebrate your successes.

A positive outlook can be contagious and can help you maintain your positive attitude. The people in your inner circle should have goals, ambitions, and a strong work ethic. Friends who are motivated and working toward goals are good role models and can encourage and inspire you to achieve your goals.

Friends in your inner circle should also have the self-confidence to celebrate your success. If your friends can't celebrate your success, they are not your friends. Avoid people who are insecure in their own ability or who are constantly minimizing the accomplishments of others.

Let me end this section with some inner-circle advice that I give to college freshmen. When you start college, you will undoubtedly encounter a few students who are always going to parties, skipping class, and bragging about all the fun they have. Don't get too attached to these students; they will soon flunk out of college.

Key points from chapter 2:

1. You can control your attitude, even if you can't control your circumstances.

2. A positive attitude contributes to productivity.

3. A positive attitude provides emotional buoyancy.

4. Manage your thoughts, and don't create unnecessary stress.

5. Address difficult situations sooner rather than later.

6. Your positive attitude is gift to others and benefits you.

7. A negative attitude will limit you.

8. Effective leaders see opportunities where others see problems.

9. Effective leaders never settle for less than their best.

10. Fill your inner circle with people who inspire, encourage, and support you.

# Chapter 3: Balance Your Life and Keep Learning

Take a minute and think about what is important to you. Likely, you are thinking about different areas of your life: family, friends, goals, school, work, volunteering, etc. "Life balance" refers to the ability to focus effort and energy in each important area of your life.

Generally, you are more successful and happier when your life is in balance. Conversely, if your life is not balanced, productivity and happiness can be difficult to sustain. Finally, realize that if your life is out of balance, the effects are probably felt by those people you care about the most.

## A Balancing Act

Success requires a focus on priorities, but it's possible to focus too narrowly. I used to define success narrowly as "success at work." During that time, my health suffered, and I was not spending quality time with my family. Success at work is good—but not at the expense of other important areas of your life. Truly successful people invest time and energy in each of the important areas of their lives, and they don't sacrifice life balance pursuing "success."

In the space below, describe what "living a successful life" means to you:




A balanced life fosters contentment, but an out-of-balance life can be stressful when you realize you are neglecting some important areas of your life. A balanced life allows achievement in several areas. Finally, your ability to dedicate time to each important area of your life can inspire others to see themselves living a successful life.

Below is an exercise that can provide insight into your life balance. Refer to table 1 as I describe this exercise. (This table is also available on my website.) I have listed several potential areas of importance in your life, and you can tailor the list to suit your needs.

First, rank the importance of each area listed as Very Important, Average Importance, or Not Important. At this point in your life, everything may seem important. You don't have unlimited time, however, so you must decide what is *most* important and invest your time accordingly.

Second, estimate the time you currently spend in each area as Too Much, Just About Right, or Not Enough. Then, for the next three or four weeks, track the time you spend in each area. Of course, the amount of time spent in each area does not tell the whole story; be sure to evaluate the impact you are having in each area, as well as the time you invest.

Finally, assess your results and reflect on the following questions:

1.  Did your original estimate of "Importance" and "Time Spent" in each area match how you spent your time?

2.  If not, what changes are needed?

Use the information you gained in this exercise to develop and implement an action plan.

Let's look at a couple of examples. Consider a person who listed "Exercise" as "Average Importance" and has a goal to exercise an hour a day. The time log shown in table 1 revealed that the person exercised five hours per week, falling short of the seven-hour weekly exercise goal. The action plan is to increase the exercise frequency to one hour per day.

Consider someone who listed "Family" as "Very Important" but discovered they need to dedicate more time for their family. The Action Plan, of course, is to spend more time with family. As you complete this exercise, be sure to put specific activities in your plan. In this example, the specific activity is taking your little sister to a movie.

Life balance requires continuous monitoring and deliberate effort, but the benefits of a balanced life are well worth the effort. Repeat this life-balance exercise over the next few months, then consider the following questions:

1.  Are you truly investing your time in each of the important areas in your life?

2.  Do you have more peace and contentment as you balance your life?

3.  What is the most important thing you learned from this exercise?

**Table 1.** Life-balance worksheet.

| Area | Importance | Estimated time spent | Actual time spent | Assessment | Action Plan |
|---|---|---|---|---|---|
| Exercise | Average | Not enough | 5 hr./wk. | Need more exercise | 1 hr./day |
| Family | Very | About right | 3 hr./wk. | Need more family time | Movie with Sis |
| Friends | | | | | |
| Goals | | | | | |
| Hobbies | | | | | |
| School | | | | | |
| Sleep | | | | | |
| Social media/gaming | | | | | |
| Spirituality | | | | | |
| Sports | | | | | |
| Time alone | | | | | |
| Volunteering | | | | | |
| Work | | | | | |

# Live and Learn

In addition to life balance, successful people commit to lifelong learning. When I graduated from college with my bachelor's degree, I felt I knew less than when I had started college. I learned a lot as a student, but I also learned that I still had a lot to learn. When I finished my PhD program, I had a deep understanding of a lot of things. Again, however, as I began my career, I quickly learned that I still had a lot to learn. I've been out of graduate school for more years than I care to count, and I continue learning. Commitment to lifelong learning is critical to your continual progress and is a key characteristic of leaders who conquer increasingly difficult challenges.

Not only will future challenges be increasingly difficult, but they may not exist today. A colleague of mine tells a story about a speaker who told students in his high school class that many of them would work in careers and face challenges that currently didn't exist. My colleague said he did not believe the speaker at the time, but now knows the speaker was correct. Consider this example: Careers in social media that exist today did not exist a few short years ago. You are preparing to address issues and work in careers that currently don't exist. Therefore, you must embrace lifelong learning.

A mentor helped me understand the importance of lifelong learning. I asked him what advice he had for me as I began my career, and he replied, "No one cares what you know about nitrogen cycling (the topic of my graduate research). What is important are the skills you have learned that you can apply to other research topics." I was shocked to hear what he said. I had spent six years working a ridiculous number of hours reading research papers, conducting research experiments, and publishing manuscripts. I had pulled all-nighters and worked on weekends, evenings, and holidays. And nobody cared about what I know about nitrogen? That was what I had heard—but that was *not* what he had said.

My mentor was telling me that my education was not over when graduate school ended, but was, in fact, beginning. I could not rely solely on what I had learned in the past, but I needed to keep learning and leverage my skills to increase my ability to solve new problems. In short, I had to commit to lifelong learning. His advice has proven to be correct.

One of the most significant lifelong learning moments in my leadership life came three years into my faculty career. I was successful, and I had even received an award. I could have easily kept cruising at my current level with no real negative consequences. I realized, however, that I needed to improve my skills in order to reach my goals of significantly advancing in my career. Don't miss this point: *I had to improve my leadership and soft skills in addition to my technical skills in order to progress in my career.* Doing so required a commitment to lifelong learning. Although we are focusing on leadership and soft skills here, technical skills are very important to your career success and must be continually developed.

Lifelong learning requires a conscious effort. Recognize this fact and look for and take advantage of opportunities to learn. If you are complacent or if you are merely not looking for the chance to learn, excellent opportunities will pass you by. Although you may not be disadvantaged directly, you will lose a chance to grow.

Let me illustrate this point further with a sports analogy. Winners in sports are those who gain an advantage, if only for a brief time. Have you ever seen a basketball team go on a "ten-two run" in five minutes and then win the game by seven or eight points? The victory goes back to that brief five-minute period when they gained an advantage.

You want to gain a similar advantage in life, and you can by committing to lifelong learning and engaging in the right opportunities. As discussed in the section called "Challenge Yourself," successful people deliberately look for opportunities to learn. Realize that engaging in a single opportunity can set you on an entirely different trajectory for your life. I wish I would have understood that concept when I was younger.

Let me share an example to illustrate the impact of a single opportunity. I advised a leadership development program for college students for several years. Although the program greatly enhanced the professional development of dozens of young people, the impact on one young man stands out. Even though his apparent leadership ability lagged in comparison to that of his peers, he took a risk and applied for admission to the program.

The leadership program gave him the opportunity to develop his success skills. He worked hard by dedicating himself fully to the assignments and became one the most accomplished students in the program. He earned the respect of his peers and graduated from college. Furthermore, he continued his education and earned a master's degree.

The student set aside his doubt and took a risk. He took advantage of a learning opportunity, and that opportunity changed the trajectory of his life.

Key points from chapter 3:

1. Successful leaders balance their lives.

2. Life balance yields contentment and fosters success.

3. Deliberately invest quality time in each area of importance.

4. Repeat the life-balance exercise regularly.

5. Problems change. Solutions change. Opportunities change.

6. You are preparing to work in a career that may not currently exist.

7. Constantly improve your current skills.

8. Develop new skills.

9. Take advantage of every opportunity to learn.

# Chapter 4: Maintain the Proper Context

Context serves as a frame of reference, provides motivation for your activities, and keeps you focused on your priorities. Maintaining the proper context prevents you from getting so caught up in what you are doing that you lose sight of your overall goal. Further, context greatly influences the way you see your activities and your setbacks. The material in this section can make a tangible difference in your success journey, if you understand and apply it.

## Keep Your Eyes on the Prize

Let me share a story that illustrates the concept of "keep your eyes on the prize." When I was an assistant professor, my goals were attaining tenure and promotion to the rank of professor. Achieving these milestones of advancement in higher education would position me for future opportunities. Achieving these milestones required several accomplishments, one of which was publishing my research. And publishing my research required that I run statistical analyses on my data.

One day, I found myself especially frustrated with statistics. I thought about how much I disliked statistics and asked myself a question: "Is this what my career is about? Running statistics all day?" Of course, the answer was "No."

I had taken my eyes off the prize of my goals. I had focused on statistics, which was a boring activity I did not like. Doing so caused great frustration. I developed a bad attitude, and I certainly was not productive.

My attitude and productivity improved dramatically when I regained the proper context. I was statistically analyzing my data so that I could publish my research, and the publications were required for my goal of achieving promotion and tenure. My point: Keep your eyes on the prize of your bigger goals and avoid losing the context of what you are doing by focusing narrowly on your daily tasks.

You may not be trying to publish your research to attain tenure, but if you have ever felt frustrated with your current activities or if you have gotten tired of doing something, the concept applies to you. Perhaps you have said:

1. "I am tired of my math class."

2. "I don't like writing lab reports."

3. "I don't want to study for another test."

4. "I don't want to do any more homework."

The frustration you experience likely is caused by focusing too narrowly on your current activities. Seeing your activities in the context of your bigger goals is the key to decreasing frustration and increasing motivation. For example, consider a student who has the goal to earn a business degree but who is frustrated because he doesn't like his math classes.

Business students are required to take math classes, so the frustrating math classes are contributing to his goal of earning a business degree. Thinking of the class in the context of his degree should enable the student to ignore the short-term frustration and motivate him to work hard.

What if your current activities are not contributing to your bigger goals? Then you need to re-evaluate whether you should be spending time on the activities. Successful leaders invest time only in activities that align with their goals.

Let's put this concept into action. Make a list of your current activities. Can you see these activities contributing to a bigger goal? If not, consider eliminating the activity.

Activity: Frustrating math class
Goal: Business degree

Activity:
Goal:

Activity:
Goal:

Activity:
Goal:

## Down But Not Out

Context also is important in terms of handling your daily trials and tribulations. I have not succeeded at everything I attempted, and you may not always succeed, either. When you have a setback, or fail to achieve a goal, it's easy to feel very frustrated and think that you will never get through it. If you keep the setback in context, however, you can more easily handle it and move on.

Please understand that your life is not defined by one bad grade, by one failed course, by one failed project, by one missed opportunity, by one loss at a competition, or by one poor performance on the job. When you do come up a little short, you must make a choice. If you choose to focus on the setback, you can become frustrated and disappointed. Focusing on your setbacks will take a toll on your confidence, and you may be afraid to try again or move ahead.

If you choose to keep your setbacks in the proper context, however, you can learn from your setbacks but not be intimidated by them. That D I got in college chemistry nearly caused me to quit college. At the time, I would never have guessed that I would get a PhD, become a successful university professor and leader, or start a business in which I train young people to succeed in school and on the job. If I can overcome a setback, you can overcome your setbacks, as well.

If you need some additional encouragement and inspiration, ask a few people to tell you about how they overcame a setback. You might be surprised by the setbacks encountered by the people you know. Ask what happened. Ask if they thought they would ever get over it. Ask what they learned, and then learn from their experiences.

Maintaining the proper context is an extremely valuable tool in your success toolbox. The next time you find yourself stressed or frustrated with your daily activities, remember that you are working toward big, impactful goals. Achieving your goals takes time and requires many steps, some of which, frankly, will be quite monotonous.

And the next time you have a setback, remember how I went from a D to a PhD. Your setbacks can empower you to grow and develop new skills and perspectives, if you see your setback as an opportunity, rather than a miserable end. How do you do that? By keeping the setback in the proper context, of course.

Key points from chapter 4:

1. The proper context provides reference, motivation, and focus.

2. Stay motivated by seeing your current activities as contributing to your overall goals.

3. Your life is not defined by a setback or failure.

4. Learn from your setbacks and move ahead.

5. Successful people remain fiercely committed to their goals.

# Part II: Relationships

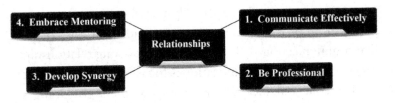

To succeed, you must be competent, and you also must work effectively with others. Both are important. I have worked with some very gifted scientists who were poor collaborators. They were smart, but they could not get along with others. Conversely, I have worked with some wonderful people who were not very competent. They were nice, but they could not perform their job duties adequately. I also have worked with countless individuals who excelled at their jobs and were great people with whom to work. Successful people excel in the competence of their chosen field and also create and maintain relationships.

Furthermore, relationships yield a network of friends and contacts. Networking often provides leads for jobs and resources for solving problems, both of which can greatly enhance your success. Perhaps you have heard the expression, "It's not *what* you know, but *who* you know that is important." Networking is about who you know.

The overall quality of your life often mirrors the quality of your relationships. If you are not as happy, productive, or fulfilled as you would like to be, take an inventory of your relationships. Invest time in your relationships that are not as strong as they could be. Surround yourself with people who inspire, encourage, and support you. And be sure that you are a positive influence on your friends. Ultimately, it is our relationships with others that truly matter.

Our discussion of relationships includes effective communication, professionalism, synergy, and mentoring. Effective communication skills are essential for strong relationships. A key to effective communication is focusing on your audience so that your audience understands your message. Doing so requires clarity and an understanding of what is important to them. Furthermore, effective communicators are good listeners. They also encourage and show appreciation. Effective leaders must be effective communicators.

Professionalism is another key aspect of building effective relationships. A professional is a person who is competent and is an effective communicator. Professionals see beyond differences and can work with diverse groups of people. Professionals are strongly committed to high integrity, and they follow through on their commitments. When your integrity is high and you follow through, people around you quickly learn that they can trust you. Trust is foundational to effective relationships.

Synergy is an outcome of effective relationships and refers to the ability of people working together to achieve more than if they had worked individually. Synergy is amplified in teams that are diverse in expertise, perspective, and experience. Synergistic teams know who (X) is responsible for doing what (Y) and by when (Z) it is to be completed.

Synergistic relationships require each person to work on his or her responsibilities. Leaders delegate tasks that others can do so that the leader can focus on activities only she can do. Team members refrain from delegating work upward, and they take a few potential solutions when they take a problem to the boss.

We end our discussion on relationships with mentoring. An effective mentor can help you make wise decisions, develop skills, and work through obstacles. To benefit from mentoring, be willing to listen and apply what you learn. Furthermore, you can mentor others by sharing your experience with them.

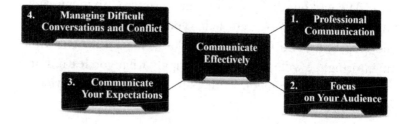

# Chapter 5: Communicate Effectively

Effective communication skills are important for your relationships, and for your success in the classroom and on the job. However, despite the importance of communication skills, employers often report a lack in college graduates of soft skills in general and of communication skills in particular.

Hart Research Associates (2015) surveyed four hundred employers, and reported that over 80 percent of the respondents ranked written and oral communication skills as very important. The survey also showed that less than 30 percent ranked college graduates as well prepared in written and oral communication skills.

Developing the mechanics of your communication skills is important but is beyond the scope of this book. Prioritize development of your writing and speaking skills by enrolling in written and oral communication courses at your school. As discussed in the section called "Academic Success Resources," college students can improve their communication skills by utilizing the resources available at the writing center on campus. Further, the Online Writing Lab at

Purdue University is an excellent resource and can be accessed at https://owl.english.purdue.edu.

Please keep in mind that although the grammar/spell-checkers in word processing programs continue to improve, the checkers are not perfect and do not substitute for well-developed writing skills. I once typed the formula for sodium bicarbonate, $NaHCO_3$, into my class notes; my spell-checker recommended I change the formula to "nacho." (Definitely a cheesy recommendation.)

## Professional Communication

Professional communication with teachers, coworkers, customers, and employers differs from informal communication with family and friends. Clarity of content, context, and intent is key to effective professional communication. Content, of course, is the message you want to communicate. Context helps your audience understand the "background" of your content, and intent lets your audience know the reason for your communication.

Clear communication requires deliberate effort and a focus on the little details that make a big difference. Let's consider an example of a student council president following up on some tasks she delegated at a recent meeting. The president could send a vague text to one of her officers: "Hey, man. Ya get that done?"

Maybe the officer will understand what she is asking or maybe he won't. Is she asking about a chemistry lab report, a math assignment, or something else? Without clear context and intent, the content can be vague.

Here is a clarified example: "Keegan, at the last student council meeting, you agreed to find three local businesses to donate items for our charity auction. [Context.] I am following up to ask if you have gotten the donations. [Intent.]"

This simple example illustrates the importance of clarity and ensuring that your recipient understands the context and intent of your communication.

Students should realize that their teachers often interact with dozens of students. If you attend a large high school or university, your teacher may instruct two or three hundred students—or more. Thus, your teacher may not immediately recognize the context and intent of your communication. Clarity can make your communication more effective.

Professional communication should be direct, as well as clear. Communicating directly can be a little intimidating for some people. But leaders have the courage to step up and say what needs to be said. Professionals express their opinions, challenge ideas, and provide constructive criticism without creating conflict. (Advice for doing so is provided below in "Managing Difficult Conversations and Conflict.")

Let's end our professional communication discussion with an example of *unprofessional* communication. I was once invited for a job interview. Upon arrival, I was informed that I was not qualified and was asked why I was there. Suffice it to say, I got mad. I got defensive and raised my voice. I already was stressed about the interview, and now I felt disrespected. I felt justified in reacting like I did. After all, I was a victim of an injustice, right?

What can we learn from this experience? First, my communication was unprofessional. Effective leaders should always communicate professionally. Effective leaders (and people in general) should control their emotions and actions: a process known as self-regulation. I, however, reacted to my first impulse without thinking.

Remember, nobody can *make* you mad. I *chose* to get mad, and nothing good came out of it. The moral of the story is that you should take personal responsibility for your actions, regardless of the circumstances. You don't have to be unemotional, and you certainly don't have to let people mistreat you. But understand that self-regulation is a key soft skill. Think before you respond.

## Focus on Your Audience

There is a saying in education: "Students don't care what you know until they know that you care." I believe the same principle applies to communication. Effective communicators convey authenticity and genuine concern for their audience. Try to understand the perspective of your audience, and communicate so your audience understands and benefits. In other words, *focus on your audience rather than on yourself.*

I learned this truth by totally missing it. I once gave a presentation to a large audience on environmental issues. The goal of the people in attendance was to learn something that would make them more effective in their jobs. I spoke to impress them, however, with what I knew, rather than communicating a message that would be of value to them. I was motivated by arrogance, rather than by concern for the audience. I succeeded in giving a very complicated presentation, but I failed miserably in providing information that was of practical value to them. I was focused on making myself look smart, and focusing on me was a mistake. Successful leaders communicate effectively by focusing on the audience and by crafting the message for their benefit and understanding.

Effective communicators listen actively and strive to understand. Active listening requires your complete attention.

Improve your active listening skills by focusing on the conversation at hand, and don't let your mind wander. Paraphrase and summarize the conversation to confirm that you understand. Ask questions. Doing so sends the message that you care enough to listen.

We often listen with the objective of making comments or solving problems. These objectives can be admirable, but often, the person speaking simply wants to be heard. In other words, the purpose of a conversation may be to allow him to synthesize and express his ideas. He may not be looking for your opinion; he will ask for your opinion if he wants it. Don't underestimate the value of simply letting someone talk to you while he or she has your undivided attention.

The following is a listening exercise I was taught at a communication workshop. Try this exercise with a partner: One person speaks for thirty seconds, while the other one remains completely silent. Then switch. Repeat using durations of one, two, and three minutes, and then discuss these questions with your partner:

1. What did you learn from this exercise?

2. How did you feel when you were listened to?

3. What nonverbal cues did you observe in yourself and in your partner?

4. What were your greatest challenges in simply listening? Be aware of these challenges and work to minimize them.

To become an effective communicator—and a person other people want to be around—learn to listen actively without interrupting. Please understand that finishing another person's sentence is an interruption. Interruption is unprofessional. When you interrupt someone, you send the message that what he says is not important. Taken to the extreme, the person you interrupt can feel that you are rude and/or that she is not important to you.

Consider a student interviewing for a scholarship. How successful would the student be if he continually interrupted the folks who are interviewing him? Not so much. Rather than interrupting, wait for a natural pause in the conversation, and then share your thoughts. If you tend to interrupt others, commit yourself to eliminating this communication error.

Interruption is an obvious verbal communication error. Nonverbal communication errors are also common, and effective communicators watch their nonverbal cues. Perhaps you have experienced speaking to someone who is texting, frowning, drumming his fingers on the table, or looking around. What do these nonverbal signals indicate? The signals send the message that although this person may *act* like he is listening, he is bored. Be aware of your body language and refrain from sending the wrong message.

Conversely, positive nonverbal communication signals convey interest and attentiveness. These positive signals include maintaining eye contact, leaning toward the person you are communicating with, and nodding reassuringly. Smiling at the appropriate time is a positive nonverbal communication signal. Notice the term "appropriate": If your college roommate is telling you about flunking an important test, smiling probably won't convey a positive signal.

Watch your nonverbal communication and that of others over the next few days. Record your observations to the following questions:

1. What nonverbal communication cues did you observe?

2. What did the nonverbal cues communicate to you?

Finally, effective leaders communicate encouragement and appreciation. The impact of encouragement was driven home to me when I spoke with a student who had flunked one of my courses. When she took the course again, I ran into her in the hallway after the first day of class. She immediately looked away and appeared embarrassed when she saw me. Her entire demeanor changed when I said, "Ya know, I had to repeat a class when I was a college student." She looked directly at me, and I could see the surprise on her face. She smiled and said, "Thank you, Dr. Green." I am proud to say she eventually earned a PhD. Make a point to encourage others. (Incidentally, this story provides another example of a student who flunked a college class but moved past the setback to earn a PhD. Don't let your setbacks stop you!)

Appreciation, too, is a powerful force influencing the attitude and motivation of people. When I was in graduate school, I got up at four o'clock one morning to help a fellow student with his research. We drove three hours to the research site, immediately got rained out, and drove three hours back. Another graduate student and I discussed that we felt taken for granted and that our effort to get up early and travel six hours was not acknowledged or appreciated. On the following weekend, we had no intention of helping. Our boss had other ideas, however, and we indeed went back to help. We got the work done this time. But more importantly, the graduate student in charge said very sincerely, "Guys, what can I say? Thank you. I could not have done this without your help." I have never forgotten how much my attitude changed when shown sincere appreciation. Always say "thank you" and show sincere appreciation to people who help you and contribute to your success.

## Communicate Your Expectations

Unmet expectations can cause conflict, often because the expectations are poorly understood and/or are unrealistic. Expectations should be communicated clearly to minimize confusion and conflict. I once asked one of my graduate students for some data I needed to finish a report. A few days went by, and I had not gotten the data. The fact that I had not gotten the data I needed made me mad. (More correctly, I *chose* to get mad at my student.) I soon realized, however, that I hadn't given my student a deadline; I had only said I needed the data. Apparently, I had assumed she could read my mind and that she would get the data to me by the time I needed it. She did not miss my deadline; she didn't know there was a deadline.

Communicate your expectations by defining X by Y by Z: what needs to be done (X), who will do it (Y), and the deadline (Z). In the missing data example, I should have defined Z by giving my student a specific date to provide the data. If you are given a task to accomplish, be sure you know the deadline. If you don't know, ask.

Clearly asking for what you want is another key to effective communication. Have you ever wanted something and were disappointed that you did not get it? If so, did you ask for it? Of course, you won't always get what you want, but I think you will be pleased by how often you get what you want simply by asking.

An uncomplicated example of asking for what you want comes from my days in Little League baseball. I wanted to pitch, but my coach never gave me a chance. I resented my coach for not letting me pitch. I assumed he thought I could not pitch. But in reality, I had never asked if I could pitch. One day, I asked, and I pitched. The rest is history—an incredibly average career as a Little League pitcher.

This childhood example provides some valuable lessons for aspiring young leaders. The key point is that I asked for what I wanted, and I got it. Furthermore, I learned that I had wrongly resented the coach for not letting me pitch. Remember, we talked earlier about the importance of demonstrating a positive attitude. We should not make the wrong assumptions. I resented my coach, and that resentment was based entirely on the wrong assumption.

Avoid this situation by asking for what you want. Perhaps you wanted to be nominated to be an officer in a club, to be on a team, or to take on leadership responsibilities—but were never asked. You may have then been disappointed or even resented that no one asked you. Don't wait for someone to ask you. Instead, ask for what you want.

In the space below, list three things you want but for which you have not asked. Make a commitment to ask for them.

1.

2.

3.

Effective leaders ask for they want. I have found that many people are happy to help if asked. Leaders benefit from asking for what they want. Asking increases the likelihood of getting what you want, which can increase your efficiency. As a leader, you can discover hidden talents in your team members, and asking can get your team members involved in your activities.

## Managing Difficult Conversations and Conflict

Let's shift gears in our communication discussion to talk about difficult conversations and conflict. Difficult conversations and conflict can focus on performance, behavior, or productivity, and, as just discussed, conflict often arises because of poorly communicated expectations. Effective leaders quickly address conflict. Doing so prevents unresolved conflict from getting worse.

Effective leaders discern the underlying source of conflict and seek to resolve it. Understanding the underlying source of conflict requires clear communication and an understanding of the conflict from the perspective of those involved. Successful resolution requires that each person specifically and honestly tell his or her side of the story and also take responsibility for his or her part of the conflict.

And each person must articulate his or her preferred solution. You are merely complaining if you can't articulate your preferred solution, and it is doubtful that you will see improvement. Your preferred solution should be specific.

For example, when students have come to my office to vent a frustration about a class or other issue, I have asked, "What is the specific problem you want to discuss?" I have also asked, "From your perspective, how should this be fixed?"

If a student tells me that he does not like a class, there is not much I can do about that. If, however, the student says that the teacher always keeps the class five minutes too long, which causes him to be late for his next class, or that homework and tests are not returned in a timely manner, then something specific can be addressed. Remember our earlier discussion on the importance of clarity in communication? Clarity is especially important for conflict resolution.

The following questions can provide insight into the conflict from the perspective of the other person:

1.  Why is this issue important him?

2.  What does he stand to gain or lose?

3.  What is his background and understanding?

4.  Do you know something he doesn't?

5.  Does he know something you don't?

6.  What is his preferred solution?

Look for common ground that you can agree on, such as facts or outcomes. It's not uncommon to be involved in a difficult conversation and realize that you and the other person may agree more than you think. If you start by finding common ground and move forward from there, subsequent conversations will be easier.

Several years ago, I served on a committee that was to determine the advising model used by a university. Two different advising models emerged after several hours of heated discussion. Debating continued until a wise person suggested that we focus on the common ground of effective advising. Looking through the lens of effective advising, each side began to see the potential benefits of the other model. We finally agreed that each model was acceptable and that colleges within the university could choose the model that best fit its students and advisors. Focusing on our differences yielded arguments, but focusing on common ground yielded a win-win solution.

As this advising example shows, conflict resolution can require flexibility and a willingness to compromise. Flexibility and a willingness to compromise do not mean, however, that you should sacrifice your values or integrity.

Navigating conflict and difficult conversations requires that you understand yourself and that you stay aware of your biases. A conflict may be rooted in the dislike of the person, rather than the issue at hand. For example, consider a conflict between the president and vice president of a student organization. Perhaps the VP is jealous because he was not elected as president. If so, the VP may constantly argue with the president regarding her ideas—not because the ideas are bad, but because the VP is upset that he did not get elected as president. The unresolved issue is that the VP has not gotten over the election results. Left unresolved, the underlying issue will lead to ongoing conflicts. Resolving the underlying issue may require a conversation with the others involved, or it may require a person to simply get over it.

Finally, resolutions require commitment and accountability. Each person must follow through on the decision that was made. If not, the person needs to be reminded that he is not doing what he said he would do.

Of course, issues addressed in difficult conversations are not always resolved completely. Strive to reach an agreeable outcome, however, even if you simply agree to disagree. This outcome provides the needed closure and should diminish the likelihood of the situation getting worse. For example, you and your roommate may not agree on what music you listen to in your dorm room. Rather than continually arguing about it, however, you can simply agree that you don't like the same kind of music. The music you listen to may not change, but at least you can stop arguing about it and move on.

Now that we have talked about things you should do in a difficult conversation, what are some things you should *avoid* during a difficult conversation?

1. Avoid accusatory "you" statements. For example, "I don't understand" is less confrontational than "You are not making any sense."

2. Don't make things personal. Try to separate the issue from the person. If your college roommate leaves his clothes all over your dorm room, talk about the fact that the room is messy (i.e., the issue) rather than calling your roommate a "lazy bum." If you have trouble with that, evaluate your motives. Similarly, challenge a suggestion made by a person, rather than challenging the person himself.

3. Don't take things personally. This can be tough, especially if the person arguing with you is trying to make it personal.

4. Don't become defensive. Defensiveness is a common reaction during difficult conversations. It's something to guard against, particularly if you know that somebody can easily irritate you. Remember self-regulation.

5. Don't immediately dismiss the perspective of the other person. The person you're having the conflict with may be right. The proposed solution you don't like may be the best solution.

6. Finally, do not immediately give in. If you strongly believe in your perspective, stand up for it. You don't have to give in just because somebody challenges you. Be sure your motives are pure, your facts are straight, and your assumptions are correct.

Difficult conversations and conflict are going to come your way; if you keep these concepts in mind, you can navigate through to an acceptable outcome.

Here is one more thought to consider: When you find yourself in a conflict and are trying to "win," be sure you understand what it means to win. If you win an argument with a friend but damage or destroy your relationship, you have lost something far more important. Losing an argument is not enjoyable, but your friendship is likely more important than winning an argument. The best long-term solution may be swallowing your pride and letting the other person win.

I want to end this section on difficult conversations and conflict with another word of advice: Get your facts straight before you criticize someone. When we moved into our first house, we had trouble with the garage door opener. I called the company that made the opener and requested a service call. When service person arrived, I let him know how dissatisfied I was with his product and company. He let me vent and then explained the situation to me: Our contractor had purchased a system that was designed for a single-car garage and had then installed it in our two-car garage to save a few bucks. Unfortunately, the smaller motor struggled to raise a larger door, which created a lot of headaches for the garage door company. Obviously, I apologized for blasting him. And I learned a valuable lesson: If you are going to criticize someone, be sure you have your facts straight.

Key points from chapter 5:

1. Focus on your audience.

2. Communicate encouragement and appreciation.

3. Be a great listener.

4. Be clear in your content, intent, and context.

5. Communicate your expectations.

6. Ask for what you want.

7. Always be professional in your communication.

8. Learn how to manage conflict and have a difficult conversation.

9. Seek win-win solutions.

10. Be flexible and willing to make an ethical compromise.

11. If you are going to criticize someone, be sure you have your facts straight.

## References

Hart Research Associates. January 20, 2015. *Falling Short? College Learning and Career Success*. Retrieved July 29, 2017 from Association of American Colleges & Universities: https://www.aacu.org/leap/public-opinion-research/2015-survey-falling-short.

# Chapter 6: Be Professional

The ability to get the job done is critical for success; make no mistake about that. Competence, however, is not enough. Other aspects of professionalism are required for success. Professionalism refers to standards of behavior and performance in the workplace.

Following are a few additional components of professionalism:

1.   Professional communication

2.   Integrity

3.   Commitment

4.   Professional appearance

5.   Appreciation for diversity

# Professional Communication Revisited

We discussed in the previous chapter that communication with your teachers, coworkers, and employer should be appropriately formal and differ from the informal communication you have with your family and friends. Let's look at a few practical examples of professional communication.

Although the norms of formality are not cast in stone, "How's it going dude?" likely is too informal a question to ask your teacher or boss. Similarly, college students should address their professors as "Dr." or "Professor." This distinction is quite important to some faculty. As an aspiring young professional, it's best to err on the side of formal rather than informal communication. Refer to your teachers' website to discern the appropriate title, or look on your course syllabus.

Set up a firstname.lastname@... e-mail account specifically for your professional correspondence, such as applying for college, scholarships, internships, and jobs. Avoid e-mail addresses such as Littleprincess@... or Bullrider@... Unless you are a four-year-old girl in a preschool play or are on the rodeo circuit, these e-mail addresses are inappropriate in a professional setting.

Your e-mail correspondence should have a clear and concise subject line. For example, "schedule spring advising meeting" is more clear than "need to meet." Address your e-mail to a specific person or audience. Remember to clearly communicate your content, context, and intent. Put requests near the beginning of your message and include a deadline. Your e-mail correspondence should be written in grammatically correct, complete sentences. Don't use ALL CAPS, and avoid using acronyms.

The same standards of professionalism apply to the greeting on your phone's voice mail. Imagine that an employer calls a job applicant to schedule an interview and hears "Hey, dude. Ya missed me. I am either out partying or sleeping it off. Leave your message, and I just might hit ya back." Entertaining? Yes. Professional? No.

Professionals strive to create error-free documents. When I was a professor, I corrected grammar and other writing errors in students' tests and assignments. Invariably, some students protested, "Hey, this ain't English class." In their defense, the students were right: I did not teach English. The point, though, is that our writing represents us and "Ererrs sendz the rong messige."

Indeed, errors send the wrong message:

1.  I don't know how to write effectively.

2.  I don't care about my work.

3.  I don't pay attention to details.

4.  I am lazy.

None of these messages is flattering.

Communication errors can disqualify you from jobs, internships, scholarships, and awards. Disqualifying a person because of a few errors in an application may seem harsh, but in a highly competitive climate, "little things" can make a big difference. Consider two students who apply for a prestigious scholarship. The students have nearly identical grades, leadership experience, and service activities. One application has a few errors, however, and results in that student being passed over for the scholarship. Similarly, a single error on a resume can cost you a job interview. An error can literally cost you money.

# Never Sacrifice Your Integrity

Integrity is characterized by high moral and ethical standards and is a hallmark of professionalism. A flaw in your integrity jeopardizes your success. Conversely, if you have the utmost in integrity, people will recognize that trait and will respect you for it.

Let me share my gold-standard illustration of integrity. One evening when I was in high school, my dad was catching up on some work at home. I noticed that he was using a mechanical pencil, and I asked if I could have it. He said, "No, you can't have this. It belongs to General Motors." I thought, *Hey, it's just a pencil.* No one would notice it was missing. Plus, it was such a tiny thing in the realm of the huge corporation. I could easily rationalize him giving me the pencil. My dad, however, demonstrated that the standard of integrity is to do the right thing. Would GM have missed the pencil? I doubt it. Would anyone have even known? Likely not. But those questions need not be considered.

Failures of integrity are self-inflicted wounds. This fact was made in ethics training I received when I was in law enforcement. Our instructor said that acting unethically jeopardizes your integrity, reputation, and career, and threatens the well-being of your family. She said that you certainly would not tolerate anyone else doing something so potentially devastating to you. Why, then, would you do it to yourself?

# Commitment Is Essential

Professionalism requires that you follow through on your commitments. Every commitment. Every time. A person who follows through on his or her commitments quickly develops an excellent reputation.

The role of follow-through on managing your reputation was driven home to me during my first performance review after starting a new job. My boss surveyed the people I worked with and asked for feedback. The most common response was that I always followed through on my commitments. I prioritized following through and kept track of every commitment. Thus, I developed a solid reputation right from the start. You, too, can develop a solid reputation if you follow through on every commitment.

I witnessed a great example of follow-through while on an out-of-state fishing trip in high school. My friend Andy and I met an elderly man who offered to take us to his favorite fishing spot if we could meet him the next morning at 5 a.m. The man met us the next morning but was too sick to take us to his spot. Despite his illness, he had made a special trip to tell us that he couldn't go and to give us directions so that we could go without him.

His effort to follow through left a lasting impression on me. The man knew he probably would never see us again, so he could have ignored us with no real consequences. His standard, however, was not that he could have gotten away without following through; his standard was that he had made a commitment and was going to keep his word. That should be our standard, as well.

As an aspiring young leader, prioritize following through on your commitments. Here are a few practical examples of commitment:

1. If you say you will be somewhere at a certain time, be there at that time.

2. If you join an organization, show up and contribute.

3.  If you enroll in a class, show up and put forth your best effort.

4.  If you say you will do something, do it to the best of your ability.

5.  If your job requires you to be at work at a certain time, be there and be ready to work on time.

Perhaps you always follow through on your commitments. If so, you possess a skill that will serve you well, and I commend you. If you are like most people, however, and don't necessarily follow through on every single commitment, I encourage you to make the commitment (so to speak) to follow through on everything you say you will do.

Finally, understand that it's better to avoid making a commitment than failing to follow through. Think before you volunteer or agree to do something. Failure to follow through is detrimental to your reputation, even when your intentions are good.

Of course, you must completely understand your commitments before you can follow through. I once supervised a brilliant student who was capable of excellent work. In fact, the quality of his work often exceeded my expectations. He did not, however, honor his commitments to show up to work on time and meet deadlines. He incorrectly assumed his work was so good that he did not have to be at his desk or meet deadlines. Partial follow-through is not enough.

To develop an excellent reputation:

1.  Completely understand your commitments.

2.  Do everything you say you will do.

3. Do everything to the best of your ability.

4. Meet deadlines.

List your pending commitments, then make a deliberate plan to follow through on them:

1.

2.

3.

4.

5.

You manage your reputation by honoring commitments. You want to have the reputation that people know they can count on you and that you have integrity. If you find that you cannot fulfill a commitment, inform the person who is counting on you. Managing your reputation fosters trust, and trust is essential for leaders.

Let me share an example of the importance of managing your reputation. I once mentored a student who was smart, had a great personality, and was liked by everyone. He constantly failed, however, to keep his commitments. I had scheduled a meeting with him, and he missed it. I did not hear anything from him for a few days, so I contacted him to reschedule. He had an excuse for missing the meeting and committed to meet with me later that week. He then missed the rescheduled meeting. I talked to one of my staff and asked if the student had contacted our office regarding the meeting. The staff member shook his head and said, "You can't count on him."

The student finally showed up a few days later and tried to use his charisma to downplay the fact that he had missed two meetings. I explained to him that he had failed to honor his commitment and that he could not charm his way out of the situation he was now in. I further explained my staff member's comment on his reputation. The student seemed shocked to hear that he had the reputation of failing to honor his commitments. His realization provided a great learning opportunity. I helped him understand that, although he was smart and people really liked him, he had to honor his commitments, rather than trying to schmooze his way out of the consequences. His commitment and reputation improved significantly following our conversation.

## Dress for Success

Professionalism requires that you wear appropriate clothing. Professional attire communicates a positive message of confidence and competence. On the other hand, sloppy or inappropriate attire can be interpreted as laziness, disorganization, or indifference. You don't have to wear expensive clothing in the latest style, but your clothes should be clean, fit appropriately, and be free of wrinkles. And of course, your shoes should be polished.

There are two main categories of professional dress: business professional and business casual. Accepted norms for business-professional attire dictate that men wear a conservative, dark-colored suit (matching suit jacket and pants), a shirt with a collar, and a tie. A black belt and polished, matching shoes are also needed. Dress socks should match your shoes and reach your calf. Generally acceptable suit colors include black, grey, brown, and navy.

Accepted norms for business-professional attire dictate that women wear a dress, skirt, pant suit, or skirt (the accepted norm is that your skirt be long enough to reach just above your knee) and dress shoes.

Of course, not all employers, industries, or settings require business-professional attire, and business casual may be appropriate. Don't be fooled, however, by the term "casual"; you are to look professional even when dressing casually.

Business casual calls for men to wear dress slacks, polos, or sweaters. Women can wear slacks, skirts, blouses, and sweaters. Jeans are not acceptable for business casual, and shirts are to be tucked in.

As mentioned earlier, these guidelines are general. If you are unsure what attire is appropriate, ask someone. If you still are unsure, err on the side of business-professional dress. I once represented my department and gave a presentation at a university-wide event. I showed up casually dressed. To my surprise (and embarrassment), everyone else who spoke wore a coat and tie. I felt (and was) unprofessional.

College students who need business-professional attire to wear to interviews can check with the career center on campus. Many offer free or low-cost clothing to students.

## Work Effectively with Others

Professionalism requires an appreciation for diversity and the ability to consider opinions different from your own. Doing so can be difficult when you think you are right or when you don't respect people whose views are different from yours. Professionals put aside biases and effectively work with others. Understand that:

1. A person who is different from you can have good ideas.

2. A person who disagrees with you can have good ideas.

3. A person with whom you don't get along can have good ideas.

4. A person who constantly complains can have good ideas.

A valid comment or idea can be dismissed because of bias against the person making the comment, rather than on the merit of the comment itself. Professionals avoid this behavior, and successful leaders won't allow bias to limit their team.

Professionalism requires you to recognize that others may work differently from you. I am a very linear thinker, and I like to plan projects in minute detail. I have worked with many highly productive people who approached projects in the opposite fashion. But the key is that they, too, are capable of high-quality work. This point was driven home for me while I was participating in a national leadership-development institute. The participants were leaders from academia, government, and industry. We had taken several different assessments designed to help us better understand our work style. When the results were returned, we lined up according to styles: early-starters to procrastinators; planners to non-planners; and concrete thinkers to abstract thinkers, etc. I was surprised to see that the group spanned the entire continuum of work style and approach. The point made—and it was made well—was that there are many effective work styles. Thus, recognize that people may not work like you do, and be able to work with those people despite their differences. Be flexible and able to adapt to your team's approach.

Modern classrooms and workplaces include people from different cultures. I have always tried to treat others with respect, and I thought that was all I needed to know about working with diverse individuals. I attended a diversity workshop, however, where I learned that being nice is important, but it is not enough. Professionalism requires that you attempt to understand fellow students or coworkers who may have different religious, racial, and cultural backgrounds. Professionalism does not require that you agree with everyone, just that you are able to work effectively with people who are different from you.

Consider a couple of simple examples of differences in cultural norms. Americans generally look each other directly in the eye during conversations. In our culture, doing so suggests that you are interested and are paying attention. In other cultures, however, direct eye contact may be considered rude. So, lack of eye contact would not necessarily indicate that the person is not listening to you, but may reflect that person's cultural norm.

Cultural differences exist for personal space, as well. I have a good friend who is from another country. When he talks, he stands very close to the person he talks to. Doing so is common in his culture. Most Americans, however, generally don't stand that close. When we first met, I kept backing up as we talked, and of course, he would step closer again. As our friendship developed, we had a good laugh after realizing that we walked when we talked.

The above examples provide very simple illustrations of some common cultural differences you might encounter. A full discussion of interacting with people of different cultures is beyond the scope of this book. The take-home message, though, is that although being nice is important, you should take the time to get to know the people with whom you work or attend school, and try to understand a little bit about them. Use this understanding to enhance your ability to work with others.

Key points from chapter 6:

1. Competence alone is not enough.

2. Create error-free documents.

3. Do not negotiate with your integrity.

4. Follow through on every commitment every time.

5. Manage your reputation.

6. Make a positive statement with your appearance.

7. Consider perspectives different from your own.

8. Seek to understand your coworkers and class-mates.

9. Embrace diversity and work effectively with others.

**Develop Synergy**

1. **Synergistic Teams**

3. **Keep Responsibility Where It Belongs**

2. **Diversity Revisited**

# Chapter 7: Develop Synergy

Synergy is the increased productivity of a team relative to the sum of the productivities of individual team members, and synergy is a key benefit of teamwork. I discussed synergy with a student who read a draft of this manuscript. His questions and feedback generated additional ideas and improved this chapter. That discussion demonstrates the power of synergy: People often accomplish more when working together than when working alone.

Synergy does not occur, however, simply because people happen to be on the same team. Perhaps you have seen an all-star sports team that had great individual players but did not perform well, because the players did not play together effectively. Without synergy, teams struggle and under-perform. Team meetings are boring, and projects are completed poorly, if at all. Team members think teamwork is a drag, which is unfortunate for two reasons. First, teamwork can be very gratifying if done correctly. Second, the discussions and interactions that underlie true synergy generate better outcomes.

# Synergistic Teams

Synergy is achieved as team members show up, speak up, and step up. Synergy requires team members to share ideas and give candid feedback. Therefore, synergy demands that team members respect and trust each other. Finally, synergistic teams are diverse and include people with unique perspectives, experiences, cultural backgrounds, and expertise.

Synergistic teams engage all members. Perhaps you have attended a team meeting and witnessed one or two people dominating a discussion. Perhaps a few people said nothing. An effective leader engages all members by directing questions to individuals who are not contributing and does not allow anyone to dominate a meeting or conversation.

Synergistic teams have focused conversations. Conversations tend to spiral into irrelevant topics. For example, consider a conversation focusing on the selection of a location for a student-leadership retreat. Someone might suggest that the retreat be held at their family's lake house, and then the next twenty minutes are spent talking about skiing, fishing, and sunburns, rather than about selecting a retreat location. Effective leaders keep conversations focused.

Synergistic teams have conversations that are clear in context, intent, and content. Synergistic teams also have meaningful conversations that are direct and respectful. Team members must provide constructive criticism and challenge ideas without being confrontational. Doing so requires trust, and an effective leader ensures that all team members are heard and respected.

Finally, synergistic teams consist of members who are both self-motivated and dedicated to the team. Self-motivation drives you to perform at your highest level, and dedication to the team dictates that you do so for the overall good of the team. You demonstrate dedication to the team by supporting your team and putting forth your best effort, even when your ideas don't ultimately govern team direction. Remember the "I in Team" concept discussed earlier in the book. Use your strengths to help your team succeed.

Incidentally, putting the team first can result in opportunities for individual team members. I was active on a recruiting-and-retention team in my department. I worked hard and made contributions. Soon, I was moved to a team at the college level (one level higher than the department team). I continued to make a difference, and eventually, I was selected to lead the college team, as well as another important program. When a leadership position opened at the college level, I was promoted. That position led to a higher position at another university.

The point is that successful people perform at their highest levels as individuals, as well as team members. Doing so solidifies your reputation and positions you for future success.

## Diversity Revisited

It is tempting to build a team of people who are "just like me." Doing so, however, diminishes effectiveness. Successful leaders build diverse teams of people with unique perspectives, experiences, cultural backgrounds, and expertise. Successful leaders seek the best outcomes, and diversity in membership yields diversity of ideas. Discussions are richer, and outcomes are improved.

As a young person, don't underestimate the importance of diversity based on experience. My neighbor gave me this advice when I was in high school. He shared a story about his work as a senior member of a team; the rest of the team were well-educated but inexperienced recent college graduates. Despite their great academic training, they could not solve a problem. When my neighbor solved it, and he said the graduates looked at him as if to say, "Wow, how'd the old dude figure this out?" He told them he had learned something several years before while working on another project, and that experience had led him to the solution.

Diversity of experience is important. Recognize and appreciate the experience of those who have "been there," especially when starting a new job. (Hint: The "old guy" just might be an ideal mentor for you.)

Finally, understand that some people on your team may be difficult to work with. Be sure you are not that person.

Reflect on your best and worst experiences working on a team or collaborating with others:

1. What worked well in your best experience?

2. What problems did you encounter in your worst experience?

3. How were the problems addressed?

Write your thoughts in your journal. Have you learned anything in this book that could have minimized or prevented the problems you have encountered? If so, please send me an e-mail and tell me about it.

## Keep Responsibility Where It Belongs

Developing synergy and working effectively with others requires that you keep responsibility where it belongs. Leaders often have a natural tendency to help others, and this tendency can be an asset. It can be overexpressed, however, and may become a weakness. Leaders and team members should not automatically solve a problem or complete a task for someone.

What's wrong with solving a problem or completing a task for someone? First, doing so takes time away from your priorities, and you may not get your work done. Second, completing tasks for someone sets a bad precedent: "Bring your work to me, and I will do it for you." Third, the person does not have to learn how to solve the problem himself, which denies the person an opportunity to gain new experience and knowledge.

Keeping responsibility where it belongs includes resisting the temptation to micromanage or give too much input into how things should be done. Early in my leadership career, I gave input to two of my staff who were making a brochure for recruiting students. I reviewed a draft of the brochure and told them very specifically what words to delete, what words to add, what new picture to include, etc. As I gave my input, I noticed that the staff were quickly losing their enthusiasm for a project they had enjoyed working on. I learned the hard way the lesson that I am conveying here, and on subsequent projects, rather than telling them exactly what to do and destroying their pride in their work, we discussed a vision for what we wanted, and then I let them figure out the best way to do it. This approach worked quite well. My staff did a great job because they "owned" and took great pride in their projects. Plus, they thought of things that I had not.

As a leader, you have insight and experience that your team members may not have. Of course, you should provide input and give advice, but remember that too much input can undermine morale and suggests a lack of trust. You have the wrong people on your team if you can't trust them to complete their work without having to tell them exactly what to do. Micromanagement diminishes enthusiasm and creativity and can ultimately decrease effort.

Keeping responsibility where it belongs also requires you to think through a problem before taking it to your boss. Remember that your boss is busy, and you want your time together to be as efficient as possible. You certainly should ask for help when you need it, and you should be prepared to answer questions when you meet with your boss, like why you are stuck and what you need to move forward. Also, anticipate that your boss will ask what you recommend for potential solutions or next steps.

Although delegating tasks upward to your boss isn't recommended, delegating tasks to your team members is an effective leadership skill. I once assigned tasks to one of my laboratory workers. He listened patiently, and then he said, "If I were the boss, I would do this myself." I responded, "That is why you are not the boss." An effective leader delegates tasks that others can do, so the leader can focus effort on tasks that only the leader can do.

A word of caution here: A leader should not be "too high and mighty" but should help when appropriate. I often helped staff load recruiting brochures in the van and helped clean up after awards banquets. Doing these kinds of things is good for morale and helps keep leaders humble and in touch. An aspiring young leader should understand how to delegate without micromanaging and should also pitch in when needed.

When you do delegate tasks to your team, remember X by Y by Z and clearly communicate expectations. Once you have communicated your expectations, follow up as needed to maintain accountability and ensure that work is getting done.

But don't micromanage to the point that you kill the enthusiasm and creativity of the talented people who work with you. Finally, remember to stay out of the way.

Key points from chapter 7:

1. Synergistic teams accomplish more than individuals working alone.

2. Embrace diversity on your team.

3. Engage your team members.

4. Show up, speak up, and step up.

5. Don't squash the creativity and enthusiasm of others.

6. Keep responsibility where it belongs.

7. Prepare before you take a problem to your boss.

8. Delegate tasks that someone else can do for you.

9. Focus your efforts on the tasks that only you can do.

10. Be willing to pitch in and lend a hand.

1. Selecting a Mentor

Embrace Mentoring

2. Maximize Your Mentoring Opportunity

# Chapter 8: Embrace Mentoring

This book includes numerous examples of advice and perspective I received from people who were wiser and more experienced than I. Mentoring—the process of helping others grow by providing advice and perspective—is a powerful catalyst for developing your success skills. When you help others on their journey, you, too, can make a positive impact on their lives. Furthermore, a mentor can be a great networking contact for you.

Mentoring provides perspective, and your mentor will help you make decisions and evaluate options, without necessarily telling you what to do. Your mentor helps you see different perspectives when making decisions in situations in which there may not be a single "right" answer. When I mentor a student who is selecting a major, choosing an internship, or deciding whether to go to grad school or get a job after graduation, we often talk about the pros and cons of each choice. Doing so allows the student to make an informed decision after considering various options. Making wise decisions when faced with multiple options is a valuable skill.

In some situations, your mentor may give you very specific advice. For example, your mentor may teach effective note-taking skills or show you how to conduct a detailed procedure on the job. Whether helping you to make decisions or learn something specific, your mentor is a valuable resource.

Although mentoring relationships can be formal, they need not be. I had a very impactful conversation with a professor who gave me excellent advice that changed the way I looked at my position as an assistant professor. He told me I should publish papers on both teaching and research when I started my faculty position. I had not considered publishing on teaching at that point in my career. I took his advice and wrote a couple of publications on teaching. One of these publications was the most-read manuscript in an education journal for two consecutive months. My point: Take advantage of every opportunity to learn from others.

## Selecting a Mentor

Here are three approaches to consider when selecting a mentor. You might select a mentor based on your career goals. For example, if you want to work in the banking industry, seek a mentor from the leadership of a bank in your community. This person will have the credibility and perspective to provide insight into the banking industry and can help you understand which college degrees and courses will best prepare you for a banking career. This person also can point out key skills that are needed for a successful career.

You might select a mentor to help you develop a specific skill, such as public speaking. In this case, seek out a person who is an excellent speaker. Ask her how she prepares for and delivers her presentations. Attend her presentations and take notes on her presentation techniques. Ask her to critique your presentation skills.

Or you might select a mentor based on the characteristics of the person herself. For example, you may select a person who has unique experience or who has been especially successful in career and life. Mentors who achieved an inspirational accomplishment, who have overcome obstacles, or who have made a significant impact are excellent choices.

Below are the general characteristics of an ideal mentor. Consider this list as you identify potential mentors:

1. Genuine desire to help you succeed

2. Willingness to invest time in you

3. Ability to help you see different perspectives

4. Credibility to give valuable advice

5. Courage to be honest

6. Commitment to hold you accountable

7. Compassion to be patient

An ideal mentor has a genuine desire to help you succeed. Consider a high school student who is mentored by her boss and is trying to decide whether to go to college close to home or attend an out-of-state school. The boss may prefer that the student stays close to home so the student can continue to work. If the out-of-state educational opportunity is best for the student, however, then the boss would encourage the student to strongly consider going out of state, even though the boss would rather have the student stay. If you sense your mentor has a vested interest in a decision, get input from a few other people.

A mentor should have the willingness to invest a reasonable amount of time with you so that you can have unhurried discussions. An ideal mentor can help you see different perspectives. And remember, an ideal mentor won't always tell you what to do; rather, she will help you see things from various perspectives to enable you to make informed decisions.

An ideal mentor possesses the credibility to give valuable advice. Many well-meaning people may give you advice, but you must ensure that your mentor truly knows what she is talking about. Your mentor needs the courage to be honest, to tell you things you may not want to hear, and to help you see things you may not see. She needs commitment to hold you accountable for considering the input. Finally, seek a mentor who will be patient with you as you grapple with your issues and decisions.

List three potential mentors. Make a commitment to discuss mentoring with each of them:

1.

2.

3.

## Maximize Your Mentoring Opportunity

Once you have identified a potential mentor, don't be shy about talking to her. Even in today's fast-paced world, most people are happy to invest time in a young person who is trying to develop skills. As a conversation starter, tell your potential mentor that you are developing your success skills and would like her help. Anticipate that your potential mentor will ask what skills you want to focus on and will likely ask about your goals. If your mentor works in a career in which you want to work, ask for advice on the experiences, education, and skills needed to succeed in that career. Ask if you can "shadow" her for a day or two at work. Finally, ask about her availability for meetings. One or two hour-long meetings per month is a good start.

After selecting your mentor, commit fully to the mentoring process. Following is a list of characteristics of an ideal mentee:

1. A commitment to succeed

2. Accountability

3. Preparedness

4. Willingness to be coached

5. Courage to accept constructive criticism

6. Appreciation

Mentoring will be as successful as you make it. The best advice from your mentor won't have a real impact unless you are committed to succeed. Demonstrate accountability by thinking deeply about the input you get, and then follow through as appropriate. Be sure that you complete assignments that your mentor gives you. Further, respect your mentor's schedule by starting and stopping at the appointed time. Bring a list of questions/topics to discuss. Be sure that you have thought through these items and be prepared to discuss your ideas. Don't forget the importance of professional dress.

You must be coachable. As previously mentioned, your mentor may give specific advice on what you need to do.

More likely, however, she will help you see multiple solutions or options, rather than telling you specifically what to do. Thus, you must be willing to consider different perspectives, which can be challenging. I have worked with some young people who were committed to success but were not coachable. These students had their minds made up and did not consider the other perspectives we discussed.

You must be willing to accept feedback that may be difficult to hear. If you have selected the right mentor, the feedback will be constructive and will help you grow. Finally, show your appreciation and gratitude to your mentor for investing in your success.

Key points from chapter 8:

1. Find an ideal mentor based on your goals.

2. Expect your mentor to give you perspective to help you make decisions.

3. Be coachable.

4. Be committed.

# Part III: Results

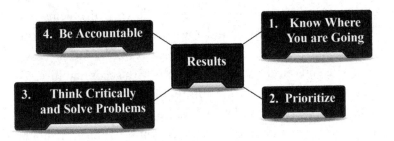

Success requires a focus on results. Producing results is different from being busy. You must understand the difference between doing something and doing something important. Many people are busy all the time but produce nothing of value. To produce valuable results, you must know where you are going, prioritize your activities, think critically, and solve problems—and you must be accountable.

Knowing where you are going means that you know your values and that you set meaningful goals. Anchoring your goals to your values is the key to setting and achieving meaningful goals. Goals that are not anchored to values are rarely achieved, or if they are achieved, the impact is small.

Prioritization is the process of focusing your time and effort on achieving your goals. Successful people understand that everything is not important. *Spending* time on things that are not important will prevent you from *investing* time in your priorities. Protect your time from urgent but unimportant activities, and don't let someone else's priorities knock you off course.

The ability to think critically and solve problems is required to produce meaningful results and achieve success. You must develop the ability to clearly define a problem and construct evidence-based solutions. Solving problems will increase your influence, and the greater your influence, the greater your potential for opportunity, rewards, and success.

We end our discussion on results with accountability. To be successful, take responsibility for your attitude, effort, behavior, outcomes, and mistakes. Be accountable to yourself, and perform at a high level. Also, be willing to take calculated risks if you want to be successful. Finally, accountability requires you to admit your mistakes, learn from them, and then move on.

4. Parable of the Garage Sale

1. The Target

Know Where You are Going

3. Setting and Achieving Goals

2. Make Success Personal

# Chapter 9:
# Know Where You are Going

Many people drift through life without any real direction or plan. These people may find success, but then again, they may not. You increase your likelihood of achieving success by figuring out what you want in life and then deliberately moving toward it. Future-orientation is the key: Invest time in activities today that benefit you tomorrow.

## The Target

The following story illustrates one of the most important principles I want you to learn. While living in Texas, I obtained my peace officer license and was a commissioned peace officer. I had the opportunity to take in-depth training on handgun shooting. For three days, we practiced several drills and developed a lot of skill. We learned the "science" of shooting, and we also developed practical skills.

We shot several qualification courses during the three days, but we had to shoot one final official qualification to pass the course. I had done very well in earlier qualifications, and I was trained, competent, and ready. We lined up and faced our targets twenty-five yards away. As we began our official qualification course, my shots were finding their target. My shooting was not perfect, but I was doing well.

Everything was great until the lieutenant said, "Cary!"

I responded, "Yes, sir?"

"You are shooting at the wrong target!"

"What?"

He repeated, "You are shooting at the wrong target!"

Well, I had two thoughts, the first of which is not repeatable here. But my second thought was, *What an incredible metaphor for life*. Despite my bruised pride, I knew I had a great story to share with young people.

Life is a lot like that experience on the range. I was trained and competent. I was getting an excellent score. But it was all for nothing because I was shooting at the wrong target. And I did not even know it—a key point. You may be so absorbed in what you are doing that you lose sight of the fact that you may be shooting at the wrong target. This can be especially difficult to recognize when you are "shooting well." Here are some examples of shooting well at the wrong target:

1. Earning good grades in a degree program that doesn't align with your strengths and values.

2. Having friends who don't share your values and drive for success.

3. Making money in an unfulfilling job.

To truly achieve success, you must shoot at the right target (i.e., your goals are aligned with your values). And then you must focus on your priorities to achieve your goals.

# Make Success Personal

Before we go too much further, let's define some terms:

1. Values are those things that truly are important to you. Values should guide your overall direction in life and provide foundational context for your goals and priorities.

2. Goals are results or accomplishments you want to achieve that align with your values.

3. Priorities are those things that preferentially receive your time, effort, and resources. Focusing on your priorities enables you to reach your goals.

For example, if you value volunteerism, your goal may be working at the local homeless shelter. You prioritize your time by working at the shelter rather than doing something else.

Because your values are foundational, determine them first. To begin, refer to the life-balance exercise in chapter 3. Also, please think back to how you described "living a successful life" in the same chapter. Expand those exercises to help you further identify your values by answering the following questions:

1. What are you truly passionate about?

2. What makes you proud?

3. What makes you happy?

4. What gives you fulfillment?

5. How would you like to be described by family and friends?

I encourage you to seek resources beyond this book as you identify your values. If you are a student, contact your advisor or counselor to identify resources available to you. Ask your mentor to help you identify your values. Additionally, you can find information online regarding determining your values.

Don't worry if identifying your values seems overwhelming at first. Your values are very important to you, and it may take time to develop a list of your true values. To provide an example, following is a list of my values:

1. My faith

2. My wife and daughter

3. Leadership

4. Excellence

5. Adding value to others

6. Health and fitness

7. Professional development

8. Production capacity

Based on what you have determined so far, list your values.

1.

2.

3.

4.

5.

## Setting and Achieving Goals

Once you know your values, develop goals based on your values. Setting and achieving values-based goals increases your likelihood of achieving success.

In the space below, develop specific goals for your values. For example, I value leadership, adding value to others, and professional development. For these values, I have the following goal: writing a book on success-skills development for young people.

Value(s): <u>Leadership, adding value to others, and professional development.</u>

Goal: <u>Write a book on success skills.</u>

Value(s):_____
Goal 1:_____

Value(s):_____
Goal 2:_____

Value(s):_____
Goal 3:_____

Now that you have set a few goals, realize that setting goals is just the beginning; you must be willing and able to achieve your goals. For example, people commonly set a goal to start a diet or exercise program on January 1. These New Year's resolutions are usually set with good intentions, but good intentions are not enough. Failing to reach a goal, even a goal set with good intentions, can cause you to get down on yourself and tempt you to abandon the goal-setting process.

Let's dig a little deeper into the influence of your values on your goals. First, your values influence whether you achieve your goals. Goals set without alignment to values are rarely achieved, because it's difficult to remain committed to something you don't care about. Your values also influence the impact of your goal. If you do achieve a goal that's not aligned with your values, the results won't have much impact. Pursuing goals unaligned with your values is an example of shooting at the wrong target.

On the other hand, goals aligned with your values are more likely to be achieved. It's easier to remain committed to something that has value to you. Achieving goals aligned with your values yields impactful results. Pursuing goals aligned with your values is an example of shooting at the right target.

Let me give a personal example. I set a goal to write my first success-skills book, *Leadership and Soft Skills for Students*. As shown above, the goal aligned with my values of leadership, adding value to others, and professional development. I worked on the book for a few years. I was tempted more than once to give up. But the goal to write the book aligned with my values, so I had the commitment to follow through.

As you grow as a leader, your goals will evolve and become more impactful, and they will be more difficult to achieve. Your commitment will be tested. Your time will become more and more precious amidst competing priorities. Armed with a true understanding of what's important to you, you will be able to set the right goals. And you will be able to stay committed to and focused on these goals.

Consider setting short-term (days and weeks) goals, medium-term (months) goals, and long-term (years) goals. Think back to my discussion of running statistics to publish my research to reach my goal of promotion and tenure. My long-term goal was to receive promotion and tenure; that goal required six years. To reach that long-term goal, I needed to write research publications, a medium-term goal that took a few months per publication. To write the publications, I needed to do several things, one of which was to run statistics. Thus, I set short-term goals prioritized on statistically analyzing my research data. As we discussed in "Maintain the Proper Context," I worked on the statistics (short-term goal) for a few days, which contributed to my publications (medium-term goal), which contributed to my long-term goal of promotion and tenure.

What might long-term, medium-term, and short-term goals look like for a college student? A long-term goal could be earning your college degree in four years. Medium-term goals include earning a 3.0 GPA this semester and completing your research paper this month. Short-term goals could be finishing your biology lab experiment and lab report this week or meeting with your chemistry tutor on Thursday.

Following are some steps to help you achieve your goals:

1. Align your goals with your values.

2. Define the outcomes of your goals.

3. Define the benefits of your goals.

4. Identify the major steps required to achieve your goals.

5. Stay focused on priorities.

6. Review progress regularly.

7. Maintain accountability.

8. Reflect and assess.

A critical first step in setting goals, regardless of their duration, is to align your goals with your values. Once you have your goals, define the outcomes and impacts of your goals by writing down what the successful completion of each goal will look like. And also write down the benefit of achieving each goal and how it relates to your values. Writing down the benefits clarifies the reason for setting the goal in the first place and serves as motivation when you struggle to keep momentum in reaching the goal. Furthermore, experience shows that written goals are more likely to be achieved. If you lose momentum, review your written impacts and benefits to motivate yourself to achieve your goal.

As you define the benefit, answer a few of the following questions:

1. When I achieve this goal, I will benefit by …

2. Achieving this goal will allow me to …

3. Achieving this goal is important to me because …

Using the example goal of my book, the following are my answers to the above questions:

1. When I achieve this goal, I will benefit by feeling satisfied that I am being true to my values. I may make some money, as well.

2. Achieving this goal will allow me to have a positive impact on young people I may never meet. Writing the book will allow me to make a greater impact than I could without the book.

3. Achieving this goal is important to me because the book should benefit the young people who read it. Plus, I have had the goal to write a book for several years; achieving this goal will be fulfilling.

Next, define the major steps. Your goal likely will require several steps. Define these steps and assign time frames for completion. Don't underestimate the importance of knowing your next steps. Perhaps you have felt overwhelmed by a mountain of tasks looming in front of you, and perhaps you were unsure of what to do next. The lack of a clear path forward can be paralyzing. Developing a list of next steps for all your projects provides a clear path forward. My mentor taught me to always know the next two or three steps for everything on which I was working. Following her advice greatly reduced wasted time, as well as frustration, because I always knew what to do next. Knowing your next steps requires that you spend time regularly planning and assessing your work, but this time is well spent.

Using the example of my book, the following is a simplified list of next steps:

1. Develop an outline for chapters.

2. Develop an outline for subheadings.

3. Write the first draft.

4. Develop figures for each chapter.

5. Solicit input from students, teachers, advisors, early career professionals, and career counselors.

6. Revise text based on input from reviewers.

7. Select a publisher.

8. Submit the manuscript to the publisher.

Once you have developed a list of next steps, get started. Be sure to review your progress regularly. If you have a goal that takes weeks or months to achieve, don't wait weeks or months to assess your progress. Periodically assess your progress, and ask yourself the following questions:

1. Am I on track with my plan?

2. What are my next steps?

3. Are there specific next steps that are behind schedule?

4. Is this goal still a priority?

5. Am I letting other things get in the way of this goal?

As discussed earlier, it is easy to lose perspective of the value of the larger goal when you get mired down in the details and activities of the steps necessary to achieve the larger goal. Review the benefits you wrote for your goals as you assess your progress. The more you reinforce the beneficial impact of the goal you are working on, the better you will handle distractions and challenges that always accompany achievement of significant goals. Sharing your written goals with someone else and being accountable to that person will also help you achieve your goals.

Finally, once you achieve a goal, reflect on the goal itself and on the process of setting and achieving goals. It's a good idea to celebrate your accomplishments and to reflect on what you learned about the process of setting and achieving goals. As you reflect, ask yourself the following questions and write your answers in your journal:

1. What worked well?

2. What didn't work well?

3. What have you learned that you can apply to your efforts to reach other goals?

## Parable of the Garage Sale

Think back to when you were younger. Think about the toy you really wanted. A new slingshot was my most coveted toy. I finally got the slingshot, and it was nice … for a while. My slingshot, however, soon ended up in a garage sale.

What about the toy *you* really wanted? Where is it now?

My point is that you may want something and spend tremendous amounts of time and effort striving for it, only to later relegate it to life's garage sale. Pursuing things that only have a short-term impact or that do not align with your values lessens your ability to reach your true goals. For example, several years ago I developed a great interest in photography. I spent a lot of time (and money) on it. Now, although I still enjoy photography, I realize that I spent too much time on it. Had I spent time on something more impactful, such as writing books, I would have been better off in the long run. Successful people pursue values-aligned goals that will have a lasting impact.

The photography example illustrates the importance of future-orientation. The key point is that you should invest your time now in activities that will benefit you in the future. Examples of future-oriented activities for high school students include:

1. Researching potential universities to attend.

2. Visiting the online career centers at several universities and going through their assessments to identify potential careers.

3. Reviewing degrees offered at several universities and identifying potential areas to major in.

4. Identifying universities you want to visit and determining how to schedule a campus tour.

Examples of future-oriented activities for college students include:

1. Searching for summer internships or study-abroad opportunities.

2. Reviewing online job descriptions to learn about education and experience requirements, as well as the duties and responsibilities for careers you are interested in.

3. Reviewing the website of the career center at your school. Be sure that you are utilizing the resources available to you.

List three future-oriented activities you can engage in:

1.

2.

3.

Key points from chapter 9:

1. Values are those things that are important to you and guide your overall direction in life.

2. Goals are results or accomplishments that you want to achieve and are aligned with your values.

3. Priorities are those things that preferentially receive your time, effort, and resources.

4. Successful people shoot at the right target.

5. Write down the outcomes and benefits of your goals.

6. Know the next steps for all your goals and projects.

7. Invest time in activities that benefit your future and will have long-term impacts.

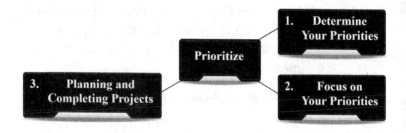

# Chapter 10: Prioritize

We may think we are making progress simply because we are busy, but this thinking is incorrect. Successful people understand that busyness does not necessarily lead to productivity. In fact, busyness can keep us from accomplishing anything meaningful by giving us a false feeling of accomplishment while stealing our time. Understanding this difference and applying that knowledge can have a huge impact on your success.

Sometimes, the difference between busyness and productivity can be difficult to see. Most people recognize common time-wasters such as spending a lot of time watching television or playing video games for hours. The difference, however, between good activities and priority activities can be more difficult to recognize. Please don't miss this point: Not all "important" activities are equal, and "good" activities can get in the way of your true priorities. Spending an entire weekend volunteering at the local animal shelter may not be the best use of your time if you have an exam on Monday. Volunteerism is a good activity, but preparing for the exam is a priority activity.

Effective time management through prioritization is essential to your success. As an aspiring young leader, *invest* your time in your priorities, and don't *spend* time on busyness. Continually assess your current activities, and eliminate time-wasters. The following questions can help you assess your skills in prioritization and time management:

1. Are you busy but not productive?

2. Do you often think you could have done better on a task if you had had more time?

3. Do you consistently miss deadlines?

4. Do you consistently ask for extra time to get your work done?

5. Do you have to pull all-nighters or rush at the last minute to get your work done?

If you answered "yes" to these questions, your time-management skills can likely be improved.

## Determine Your Priorities

Determining your priorities is *the priority* for improving your time-management skills. We discussed in the previous chapter that your values, goals, and responsibilities greatly influence your priorities, and that your priorities should have a long-term impact. Let's dig a little deeper into determining your priorities.

Health and fitness are values of mine. If I am true to my values, I will prioritize getting up early to exercise, rather than sleeping later. And I will prioritize eating a healthy lunch, rather than eating a double cheeseburger (with bacon). Achieving my goal of writing a book requires that I prioritize my time and stay focused on and committed to writing when bombarded with potential distractions.

Our responsibilities also influence our priorities. Students have the responsibility to attend class, complete assignments, and strive to learn. Athletes and band members have the responsibility to attend practices and work hard to improve their skills. Some students have the responsibility to work to pay for their education. Employees have the responsibility to get to work on time and be productive.

Finally, as we discussed in "Parable of the Garage Sale," your priorities should make a long-term impact. As you develop your success skills, prioritize activities that contribute to your future success, such as applying what you learn in this book.

Once you have determined your priorities, don't lose sight of them when bombarded with other people's priorities. Someone may bring an issue to you seeking help; this issue may be a priority for him but not necessarily for you. By working on his priority, you lose time that could be spent on *your* priorities. Of course, his friendship may be a priority, so his issue may merit your time. Please understand that I am not discouraging you from helping others; in fact, helping others should be a priority. Don't automatically place a higher priority on the requests of others, however, than on your own priorities.

For example, if you have a biology test in the morning, but your roommate wants to tell you about his new motorcycle tonight, you would be wise to suggest to him that you can talk about it tomorrow after your test. If your roommate has a more serious issue to deal with, you may have to help him out, and doing so may require you to stay up late studying for your test.

Furthermore, understand that urgent issues, whether yours or someone else's, are not necessarily important issues. Consider this question: If you have urgent activities and important activities competing for your time, which would you work on first? Some people incorrectly answer that they would first work on the urgent activities. The enthusiasm associated with urgency counterfeits itself as importance. Don't be fooled: You should work on the most important things (priorities) first, and remember that urgent issues are not necessarily important.

Imagine you are trying to finish a class project that is due in the morning. As you are working, you get a text from a friend. The urgency of the text can interrupt your work, and you may get drawn into a conversation that should wait until after you finish your project. You may not get your project done if you spend a lot of time texting. Or you may hurry through and fail to complete the project to the best of your ability.

Although you want to respond to your friend's text, you can wait until your priority work is done. You might text your friend and let her know that you will follow up after you get your work done. Avoiding the interruption is even better: Turn your phone off when you are working on something important. Small interruptions such as texts can decrease your efficiency.

## Focus on Your Priorities

For several years I taught an orientation class for college freshmen. I asked my students to describe their biggest challenge. The answer was always the same: "I don't have enough time." Perhaps you, too, have felt that you don't have enough time to get everything done. It is true that you do not have time to do *everything*. Successful people, however, make the most of their time by focusing on their priorities and eliminating time spent on non-priorities.

The importance of focusing on priorities was driven home to me by a committee that evaluated the accomplishments I made during my first three years as an assistant professor. The committee provided recommendations to help me reach my goal of promotion and tenure. The recommendation was to quit doing some of the things I was doing and focus on the aspects of my job that would lead to promotion and tenure. In other words, clarify and focus on my priorities.

Their advice did not immediately resonate with me. I was working very hard, and I thought everything I was doing was important. And in some ways, everything I was doing *was* important. Some of the "important" activities, however, would not help me reach my goal. Thus, although I was very busy and was working on important activities, I was not spending enough time on *priority* activities. I was spending too much time on committees and not enough time on research. Were the committees important? Yes, but committee work would not contribute much to my promotion evaluation. To be promoted, I needed to prioritize obtaining more research grant money and writing more research publications.

Using the target example discussed earlier, promotion and tenure was my target, and spending time on committee work was shooting at the wrong target. Even though I was hitting the committee-work target, time spent on committee work would not help me reach my goal. I was *doing things right*, but I was not *doing the right things*. Remember, being busy (doing something) is not the same as being productive (doing something important).

To accomplish your goals, you must focus on your priorities, and doing so means that you learn to say no. Saying no to some activities is as important as saying yes. A colleague of mine says, "When you say yes to something now, you are saying no to something else later."

My mentor helped me learn to say no by using the example of attending meetings. She asked how I determined whether I would attend a meeting to which I had been invited. I said that I usually checked my calendar and would attend if I was available. She helped me see that my approach was ineffective. She taught me first to evaluate the request based on my priorities and then attend only if the meeting aligned with my priorities.

Upon reflection, I discovered that I often agreed to attend meetings or take on additional work because I wanted to be helpful. Although being helpful is important, it can lead quickly to over-commitment. Before you volunteer to do something or agree to take on additional responsibilities, ask yourself these questions:

1. Is this activity a priority for me?

2. Does it align with my values and goals?

3. Is the activity part of my responsibilities?

4. Does the activity have a long-term impact?

If the answer is yes, step up and contribute. Otherwise, politely decline.

Of course, there will be situations in which you must take on additional work. Your boss may pile additional work on you. How should you handle the increased workload? Ask your boss to help you prioritize your tasks so you complete the most important tasks first.

# Planning and Completing Projects

Let's go through a practical example to help you prioritize your time and achieve your goals/ complete your projects. I use this simple process to stay organized, manage time, and stay focused on priorities. This approach builds on the outlining process described in "Setting and Achieving Goals." When you set a goal or plan a project:

1. Outline the steps needed to complete the project.

2. Estimate the time required to complete each step.

3. Determine the deadline for each step.

4. Schedule in your calendar time to complete each step.

5. Stay focused on your priorities.

6. Assess your progress and stay on track.

Be sure to adjust all deadlines so you can finish your project by its deadline. You can even build in a cushion of a day or two, just in case you need some extra time.

Refer to table 2 below as we work through an example of planning and completing a term paper. (You can download a free planning template from the Resources page at www.caryj green.com.)

I listed each step required to complete the term paper and estimated the time required for each step. I estimated that selecting a topic would take an hour. The deadline was April 15, so I scheduled an hour on April 15 to get it done. I estimated that conducting research would take six hours, and I set a deadline of April 25. I scheduled two-hour time blocks on

April 17, April 19, and April 24. Doing so provides the six hours I need to complete the research and allows me to complete the step before the deadline.

I set the duration as "NA" on steps 9 and 12. These steps are simple activities that I can complete quickly and don't require a time block. For step 9, I merely need to send an e-mail to a friend and ask her to review my draft.

To maximize the value of this system, you must accurately estimate how long it takes to complete each step. You will learn to accurately estimate your time with a little practice. Of course, making this plan is important, but commitment is ultimately required to move it from a plan to a successful outcome. Stay focused and put forth your best effort.

Table 2. Project-planning template.

| Step # | Description | Duration | Deadline | Schedule time to complete each step | | |
|---|---|---|---|---|---|---|
| | | | | | Date and Time | |
| 1 | Select topic | 1 | 4/15/2016 | Apr 15, 1-2 p.m. | | |
| 2 | Make an outline | 2 | 4/16/2016 | Apr 15, 2-3 p.m. | Apr 16, 9-10 a.m. | |
| 3 | Conduct research | 6 | 4/25/2016 | Apr 17, 3-5 p.m. | Apr 19, 1-3 p.m. | Apr 24, 8-10 a.m. |
| 4 | Revise outline | 1 | 4/26/2016 | Apr 26, 2-3 p.m. | | |
| 5 | Write first draft | 3 | 4/27/2016 | Apr 26, 3-5 p.m. | Apr 27, 10-11 a.m. | |
| 6 | Review draft | 1 | 4/29/2016 | Apr 29, 4-5 p.m. | | |
| 7 | Conduct additional research | 2 | 4/30/2016 | Apr 30, 8-10 a.m. | | |
| 8 | Write second draft | 2 | 5/2/2016 | May 1, 1-2 p.m. | May 2, 3-4 p.m. | |
| 9 | Have someone review second draft | NA | 5/2/2016 | NA | | |
| 10 | Write final draft | 2 | 5/12/2016 | May 11, 1-2 p.m. | May 12, 8-9 a.m. | |
| 11 | Final edits and final polishing | 1 | 5/13/2016 | May 13, 9-10 a.m. | | |
| 12 | Submit | NA | 5/14/2016 | NA | | |

Let me end with the time-management advice I give to students. At the beginning of each semester, add to your calendar your class schedule, work schedule, student organization meetings, and other time commitments for the entire semester. Then set aside time each week of the semester to complete your school work. You might schedule six or eight 2-hour blocks each week. Doing so will ensure that you always have time available each week to complete your school work. At the beginning of the semester, you may not know what you will have to work on during the eleventh week of the semester, but you will know that you have time scheduled to do it.

Key points from chapter 10:

1. Busyness (doing something) is different from productivity (doing something important).

2. Focus your effort on your priorities.

3. Urgent issues, whether your own or someone else's, are not necessarily priority issues.

4. Learn to say no.

5. "Good" activities can interfere with priority activities.

6. Outline all steps needed to complete your projects.

7. Assign a duration and deadline to each step.

8. Schedule work/study time blocks into your calendar and keep these "meetings" with yourself.

# Chapter 11: Think Critically and Solve Problems

Critical thinking is the process of using evidence and logic to evaluate information, construct reasoned opinions, make informed decisions, and solve problems. Critical thinkers are not fault-finders but independent thinkers who question assumptions and biases. Critical thinkers are reflective and question their own beliefs, as well as the information they encounter. Critical thinkers are creative and excel at problem-solving. Critical thinkers think independently, but remain open-minded and evolve their opinions as new evidence is discovered.

## Critical Thinking

Students who think critically are less focused on memorizing facts and more focused on learning underlying principles. These students are equipped to compose informed answers on tests and to construct evidence-based term papers and presentations.

Employers highly regard critical thinking and the ability to integrate principles and knowledge to solve problems. Further, critical thinking is important to everyday activities ranging from deciding on what phone to buy to determining which candidate to vote for.

The following tips can help you enhance your critical thinking:

1. Think independently.

2. Separate fact from opinion.

3. Ask questions.

4. Evaluate biases and assumptions.

5. Evaluate evidence.

Critical thinkers think independently. You will continually be bombarded with information and opinions. Don't believe everything you hear, and don't be influenced to act or believe something simply because others do. Develop your own views and make your own evidence-based decisions.

Critical thinkers separate fact from opinion. Facts can be proven; opinions cannot. I have a gas grill (fact), and I cook the best-tasting steaks in town (opinion). Opinions are biased at best and can be misleading or deceptive at worst.

Critical thinkers do not automatically dismiss information, but they ask questions to evaluate biases and assumptions before accepting the new information as fact. What evidence is provided? Does it make sense? How is the evidence supported? Is there reason to think the information is biased?

For example, a car dealer once told me that a car I was looking at was "perfect" for me. Is that statement a fact or just an opinion? How could he know what is perfect for me? Is there a potential bias in his statement? If I were easily swayed by his opinion, I would have bought the car right then. I asked several questions, however, and decided not to buy the car. This example is quite simple, but the concept applies to more complex situations.

Put your critical-thinking skills to use in the following exercise. Watch a debate between two people who have different opinions of an issue. You can find these discussions on news programs or online. Apply your critical-thinking skills to evaluate the discussion and answer the following questions:

1. Can you distinguish facts from opinions? Explain.

2. What evidence was presented?

3. Describe any biases you observed.

4. Which speaker was the most convincing? Justify your opinion.

5. Did your view on the subject change after listening to the discussion? Explain.

6. What did you learn about developing and presenting an opinion?

Repeat the exercise and invite a couple of friends to participate. Discuss the questions above. Did everyone reach the same conclusion? Why or why not? How will you apply what you learned?

Here is another critical-thinking exercise. Consider the following scenario, which is based on an actual experience of mine. A salesman told me, "If farmers use my product, they can cut their fertilizer rate in half without losing any yield [the amount of crop produced]." Let's use our critical-thinking skills to evaluate the salesman's claim.

To prove his claim, the salesman had set up an experiment on a farmer's field and had compared two treatments. The first treatment was the normal fertilizer rate, and the second treatment was half the normal rate of fertilizer, plus the product. The treatments were replicated three times across the farmer's field, and all other management practices were uniform across the treatments. The research plots were harvested at the end of the season, and there was no statistically significant difference in yield between the two treatments (in other words, the yields were the same).

The salesman concluded, "I proved in a replicated experiment that if farmers use my product, they can cut their fertilizer rate in half without losing any yield." Before reading further, please discuss below whether you conclude the claim to be proven. Justify your conclusion. (You need not know anything about agriculture to critically evaluate the claim.)

Did the salesman provide evidence to support his claim? Yes. The salesman provided yield data from a replicated experiment, and the data appear to support his claim. Did the salesman bias the experiment to favor his product? No. The field was managed uniformly; the only variable was the treatment itself. So far, so good.

Indeed, the salesman was convinced he had proven his claim. Are you convinced? Remember, critical thinkers ask questions to evaluate evidence, rather than automatically believing everything they hear. What questions might you want to ask?

Let's look deeper into the evidence. More specifically, let's look deeper into the *treatments*. Treatment 1 was the normal fertilizer rate, and Treatment 2 was half the normal rate of fertilizer, plus the product. A critical thinker would ask, "What yield would you get by using half the normal rate of fertilizer *without* the product?"

The salesman assumed that using half the normal rate of fertilizer would limit the yield, and that assumption needed to be evaluated by comparing yields from the half-normal rate both with and without the product. I asked the salesman about the missing comparison, and he was unable to answer my question. The salesman's claim cannot be proven without this comparison.

This example demonstrates the power of using critical-thinking skills to ferret out assumptions and evaluate the validity of evidence. Note that an understanding of agricultural science was not needed; critical-thinking skills alone uncovered the flaw in the salesman's claim.

Let's take this example a step further. Although critical-thinking skills uncovered a flaw in the salesman's claim, a solid understanding of agricultural science is needed to fully explain the results of the experiment. My knowledge of agriculture told me that the half-rate was enough to produce maximum yields, and that adding the normal fertilizer rate would not increase yield further. (Ironically, the salesman's experiment supported *my* conclusion, not his).

As you develop your success skills, be aware of the synergy that occurs as you combine critical-thinking skills with the technical/scientific knowledge of your discipline. Make a commitment to continually refine your critical-thinking skills and deepen your disciplinary expertise. Doing so equips you to solve increasingly complex problems and makes you indispensable to employers.

# Define the Problem

Critical thinkers excel at problem-solving, and the most important initial step in solving a problem is defining the problem to the best of your ability. Consider a car that won't start. You can change the battery or replace the starter, but if the problem is an empty gas tank, changing those parts will not help.

I learned the value of defining the problem while having a discussion with a colleague about my plan to increase enrollment in our college. The conversation went something like this:

| | |
|---|---|
| Me: | "Enrollment in our college is a problem." |
| Him: | "Well, what kind of a problem?" |
| Me: | "We don't have enough students." |
| Him: | "What's the problem?" |
| Me: | "We don't have enough students." |
| Him: | "Cary, what's the problem?" |
| Me; | "Well, our enrollment's not high enough." |
| Him: | "Cary, *what is the problem?*" |

After a few minutes, I realized that I was not answering my colleague's question. That conversation taught me a great lesson: You must define a problem before you can solve it. In this example, enrollment was influenced by several factors. I first needed to understand which factors needed fixing before I could solve the enrollment problem.

Consider the example of a student organization with the problem of poor attendance at meetings. How would you solve the problem? You can't solve the problem if you don't know why students are not showing up, so the first thing to do is determine why students don't attend. Perhaps students do not know when the meetings are. Maybe the meetings are boring, and nobody wants to come. Maybe the meetings are far from campus, and some students don't have cars. Perhaps the club meets at the same time as basketball practice, and many club members are on the basketball team.

Let's say that you researched the issue and found out that the basketball team does have practice at the same time you have your meetings. You could change your meeting time, and attendance should increase.

Consider another scenario: What if attendance is low because the meetings are boring, and students don't gain anything from attending? Changing the meeting time won't change the fact that the meetings are boring. To increase attendance, you would need to change the meeting agenda to make your meetings more interesting and valuable to students.

These simple examples illustrate the importance of defining the problem and understanding its underlying cause. By asking several questions and defining the problem, you will know where to start looking for a solution.

## A Six-Step Approach to Problem-Solving

Problem-solving skills can be developed, and as you gain experience, you will develop a process that works for you. The following is a simple six-step process that can serve as a framework to enhance your problem-solving skills:

1. Identify the problem.

2. Determine the underlying cause of the problem.

3. Determine possible solutions.

4. Select a solution.

5. Implement the solution.

6. Assess the solution.

In the example of the student meeting discussed previously, the problem was identified as poor attendance (step one). Before solving the problem, however, the cause of poor attendance needed to be determined (step two). Next, a few solutions were developed (step three). One possible solution was to change the meeting time due to a conflict with basketball practice. Another possible solution was to change the meeting agenda so that members could benefit from the meetings.

In the first scenario, the meeting time was moved (step four) due to the conflict with basketball practice. Changing the meeting time (step five) increased attendance (step six), and the problem was solved.

In the second scenario, the meeting time was changed (step five), but attendance did not increase (step six). The underlying cause was evaluated again, and it was determined that the meetings were boring (step two). To increase attendance, a better agenda and meeting content was developed (step three). Improving the meeting agenda (steps four and five) increased attendance and solved the problem (step six).

As you saw, the first solution (changing the meeting time) may not solve the problem. Keep in mind that to solve problems, you must think critically and creatively. Sometimes, the problem-solving approach is to plow through and do things out of habit or to try solutions that had worked earlier. For example, if the meetings were on Tuesday last semester, but are on Thursday this semester, one might conclude that changing the meetings back to Tuesday night would solve the problem. Is this conclusion an opinion or a fact supported by evidence? Does the proposed solution really address the underlying cause of poor attendance? If the meetings are boring, changing the meeting night won't help. Remember to apply your critical-thinking skills and make decisions based on fact and not on opinion.

Let's end our discussion of critical thinking and problem-solving with a question I asked my soil science students: "Consider an Alfisol that contains 2.0 percent organic matter and has a fine, sandy loam texture in the Ap horizon (surface 9 inches). How much soil is in a hole that is 7.25 cm. deep, 0.25 m. long, and 6 inches wide? State explicitly all assumptions."

Unlike my students, you may not be familiar with terms such as "Alfisol" and "Ap horizon." This problem can be solved, however, just by using the skills described in this chapter. Try to solve this problem before reading further.

Calculating the size (volume) of the hole by multiplying depth by length by width is a common approach to solving this problem. I complicated the problem by reporting dimensions in centimeters, meters, and inches. The volume can be calculated, however, by using the appropriate unit conversion factors (i.e., 1 inch = 2.54 cm., etc.)

Calculating the volume of the hole is tempting, because the calculation is reasonably straightforward, but doing so doesn't lead to the right conclusion. Clearly defining the problem before attempting to solve it is a better approach. Sorting through the distracting terms and details shows that the real question is "How much soil is in a hole?" Defining the problem solves the problem in this example because a hole, by definition, contains no soil.

Don't feel too badly if you overlooked the fact that there is no soil in a hole. After calculating the volume, many students wonder, *Geez, how could I have missed that?* This exercise reinforces the importance of truly understanding a problem before attempting to solve it. Remember that the most obvious and straightforward path to a solution (in this example, calculating the volume) may not solve the real problem. Think about your thinking process, and don't immediately chase the first solution that comes to mind.

## Parable of the Pole Position

By thinking critically, solving problems, and producing results, you set yourself up for future resources and opportunities. Throughout my career, I have seen resources given to individuals, teams, or departments who were achieving great things and did not appear to need additional resources. I also have seen resources diverted away from individuals, teams, and departments who were less productive. Why would resources go to those who were already achieving success, as opposed to those who were not as productive? Why not invest in those who are behind and appear to need help?

Resources and opportunities are commonly given to those who have the greatest potential to achieve future results. If you have been productive in the past, you probably will be productive in the future. Thus, the more successful you are, the more opportunities and resources will come your way. If your grades are good, you are more likely to get a scholarship. If your work is good, you are more likely to get a promotion. On the other hand, if you have not taken advantage of your opportunities or have not been productive in the past, you may have a hard time convincing someone to invest in you.

I refer to this concept as the "Parable of the Pole Position." Growing up in Indiana, I enjoyed watching the Indy

500. The race starts with thirty-three cars arranged in eleven rows, three cars across. The most advantageous position to be in at the start of the race is the pole position: the inside position of the first row. To determine who gets the pole position, drivers go through a series of time trials to see who has the fastest time; the fastest driver gets the pole position.

You might be tempted to think that the driver with the slowest speed should be put in the pole position to give that driver a chance. Or you might think that the fastest driver should be in the back of the field because that driver should be able to catch up. Although these philosophies may have merit in some aspects of life, success generally begets success; those who achieve the most tend to get the most.

At first glance, this concept seems like common sense, so why even bother mentioning it in this book? I include it here because I have seen several people miss this point. In fact, it took me a while to catch on to this concept when I was younger. I was used to getting things (good grades, favor from teachers, good breaks, opportunities, second chances, third chances, and so on) without much effort on my part. And that is okay when you are young. This approach is analogous to moving the slowest driver to the pole position (in other words, you get "moved up" without having to earn it).

I have seen several people mistakenly assume, however, that opportunities and resources will continue to be handed to them as they progress to college and beyond. I also had this sense of entitlement when I was young; I soon learned, however, that the entitlement of my past did not match the realities of my present and future. This contradiction took me by surprise. And I have seen many young people experience surprise, frustration, and disappointment, as well.

If you want to be successful in the future, you must earn it. The more you achieve, the more opportunities you will be given for further achievement. Don't assume that success and opportunity will come your way just because they always have. If you want a scholarship, you must work hard to get good grades. If you want a promotion at work, you must work hard and be very productive. If you assume success simply will be handed to you, you will likely find yourself frustrated as you watch others move ahead of you.

Successful people understand that success requires hard work, and they live their lives accordingly.

Key points from chapter 11:

1.  Think independently.

2.  Ask questions to evaluate information.

3.  Identify the problem and its underlying cause *before* starting to solve it.

4.  Follow the six-step problem-solving model.

5.  Remember the principle of the "Parable of the Pole Position."

# Chapter 12: Be Accountable

Successful people are accountable. Before we talk about what accountability is, let me illustrate what accountability is not. I once delegated responsibility to organize a youth retreat. My periodic check-ins led me to believe everything was on track. As the time for the retreat approached, however, it became obvious that the person I had delegated to was not following through. When I approached the person to discuss the fact that the work was not getting done, I was given an excuse that is an excellent example of what accountability is not. The person said, "You should have known better than to put me in charge."

## Accountability Counts

Accountability requires that you take responsibility for your productivity, behavior, attitude, and mistakes. Successful people are accountable for their effort and strive to be the best they can be.

If you compare yourself to others who have more natural ability or more experience than you have, you can get frustrated and think you can never accomplish what they do. This frustration can yield a negative attitude, loss of confidence, and lack of desire to put forth the effort you otherwise would.

On the other hand, if you compare yourself to others who are less talented or less accomplished than you are, you may get comfortable and never push yourself to achieve your potential. If the leading scorer on a team averages eighteen points per game and the next-highest scorer averages ten points per game, the leading scorer may be satisfied and not try to improve. If the leading scorer has the ability to average twenty-five points per game, however, then he is not reaching his true potential. By comparing himself to others, the leading scorer may not try to improve. Successful people are self-motivated to achieve their potential; this self-motivation requires accountability, self-awareness, and a commitment to improve their skills.

Accountability dictates that you avoid making excuses. Listen for excuses over the next few days. You may be surprised by how common excuses are. Excuses are common because it's easy to pass the blame for our shortcomings to someone else. For example, if I arrive late for a meeting, it's easy to say that the traffic slowed me down (someone else's fault). The truth is I arrived late because I did not leave early enough.

I have talked to many students about a poor grade in a class, and the students said, "I didn't like the professor," or, "That class was at eight a.m., and I am not a morning person." Those statements may be correct, but they are irrelevant.

I also often hear, "I'm not good at chemistry." Maybe you are; maybe you are not. But sometimes, the "I'm no good at ..." plea can be an excuse for quitting or not attempting something. Working harder and smarter until you succeed is a better approach for a young leader. If you don't understand chemistry, find a tutor. Put more time into it; work lots of homework problems. As a young leader, do not consider something to be a weakness until you have put forth your best effort.

## Quality Matters

Accountability requires that you perform at your highest level. Successful people put forth their best effort and generate quality outputs, rather than completing a task to check it off a list. I admit I have finished some things quickly just to say, "I finished it." This approach usually backfires, and I must do the work again. Furthermore, people may associate you with sloppy work, and this association torpedoes your reputation.

As mentioned earlier, we each have strengths in *some* areas but not in *all* areas, and we cannot excel at every endeavor. Successful people, however, consistently perform at their highest level and never settle for doing less than their best, even when working on tasks that are not enjoyable.

Being your best means doing your best. You are demonstrating your commitment to being the best you can be by working through this book. Take some time and reflect on your other activities to ensure that you put your best effort into everything you do. That's the way successful people approach life.

There are benefits for putting forth your best effort. First, you reach your true potential. If you are a student, please understand that there is nothing wrong with earning Bs and Cs, if that's the best you can do. But an A student should not be satisfied with Bs, and a B student should not be satisfied with Cs.

Second, putting forth your best effort will allow you to build a solid reputation with teachers, supervisors, and coworkers. And putting forth your best effort may allow you to get accepted into your *preferred* university or grad school, qualify for scholarships and/or awards, or get your preferred job or internship.

Ensuring that your work meets the needs of those who will use it is another dimension of performing at your highest level. When you are asked to complete a task for someone, think about how you can best meet the needs of the person making the request.

Consider an example of finding a hotel for a leadership retreat for a student organization. A person putting forth minimum effort might report back with a simple list: "I found four hotels." A true leader, however, would put forth their best effort and check into the details, then report, "There are four hotels in town. Only two have rooms available the weekend of our retreat. The first hotel charges $108/room and provides free Wi-Fi. The second hotel charges $99/room and provides free Wi-Fi, free breakfast, and a free conference room."

Consider another example of a boss asking an intern for five years of sales data from three competitor companies. An intern putting forth minimum effort would merely provide the boss a link to the websites of each company so the boss could look up the information herself. From one perspective, the boss got the data she wanted. This approach, however, represents a minimal amount of effort. This level of effort will likely prevent the intern from receiving an offer for a permanent position with that company.

A best-effort approach would be to summarize the data in a format the boss could use immediately. Although this extra effort may seem obvious to some, my experience is that many people will do the minimum to get by. Set a goal to exceed expectations when asked to complete a task, and you will be surprised at the positive effect this has on your relationships, reputation, and success.

Before we leave our discussion of exceeding expectations, let me point out how this approach can benefit you greatly. I often am requested to write reference letters for students seeking jobs, awards, scholarships, or admittance into law school, veterinary school, or graduate school. I write the strongest letters for those students who exceeded my expectations. In my letter, I provide details of how the student went above what was required. Such examples are often the key to receiving an award or scholarship, or gaining admittance into a program. Consider this fact: Nearly all the students who apply for these awards and programs are outstanding and have excellent records of accomplishment. The students who stand out as exceptional are those who have gone above and beyond what is expected.

## Handling Mistakes

Successful people are accountable for their mistakes. No one likes mistakes, but everyone makes mistakes. No one likes excuses, but many people make excuses when they make mistakes. No one respects people who use excuses instead of accountability. That behavior is disruptive on teams and in the workplace. Furthermore, others are rarely fooled by the excuses for very long.

So what do you do when you make a mistake? The following is a list of helpful steps:

1. Recognize you made a mistake.

2. Take responsibility for it.

3. Apologize for it.

4. Fix it if you can.

5. Take the necessary steps to ensure it does not happen again (i.e., learn from it.)

6. Move ahead.

Do not try to hide or cover up a mistake. Rather, take responsibility for it, then apologize. After you apologize, fix the problem if you can. Looking forward, take measures to ensure that you don't repeat the same mistake. People will usually be patient with you when you make a mistake if you apologize, own up to it, and fix it. Patience dissipates, however, if you continue to make the same mistake.

Finally, after you've recognized it, taken responsibility for it, apologized for it, fixed it, and ensured it won't happen again, *move on*. Don't play it repeatedly in your mind. Sometimes I bash myself over a mistake for a long time—a curse of perfectionism. When I catch myself dwelling on a mistake, I make a mental note of the lesson learned. Then I make a deliberate decision to let it go and stop thinking about it.

While we're on the subject of mistakes, keep in mind that successful people often make mistakes. At first, this fact may not make sense, because you may think that mistakes prevent success. In this context, however, mistakes are made by people who step up to challenges and take risks. Recognize that leaders often make decisions without having all the information needed to make an ideal decision. Doing so involves risk and may result in a few mistakes. Successful leaders learn from their mistakes, adjust, and continually move forward.

If you're working on a project or trying to make a decision and you're not exactly sure what to do but have a gut feeling for the next steps, trust your instincts and move ahead. Consider talking to a colleague or mentor to get a second opinion. Roll your ideas out in small steps and continually assess progress. If it turns out to be the wrong thing to do, stop, adjust, and move ahead. Furthermore, realize that the adverse effects of doing nothing may outweigh the adverse effects of making an occasional mistake.

I'm not glorifying making mistakes. You may not get a second chance when you make a mistake in judgment or in ethics. I know of a very tragic case of a young man who tried drugs once—just once—and that one time cost him his life. Mistakes are going to happen, though, and the best thing to do is own up to them, learn from them, and relentlessly move forward.

Key points from chapter 12:

1. Always put forth your very best effort.

2. Set a goal to exceed expectations.

3. Be accountable for your mistakes.

4. Learn from your mistakes and move on.

5. Be willing to take calculated risks.

6. Don't let the fear of mistakes hold you back.

# Part IV: Academic Success Skills

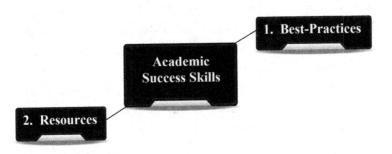

As we previously discussed, skills in time management, goal setting, communication, critical thinking/problem-solving, and accountability contribute to academic success. Here, we will discuss additional skills that contribute directly to academic success.

I define academic success as "performing at the level of your academic ability." Performing at the level of your academic ability does not require you to get straight A's. Performing at the level of your academic ability means that your academic performance is not limited by factors within your control. Performing at the level of your academic ability requires that you put forth your best effort, use academic best-practices, and utilize the academic resources available to you.

I define academic success skills as "techniques and actions that enable you to perform at the level of your academic ability." Well-developed academic success skills are essential for students. Conversely, poorly developed academic success skills can limit you. As discussed earlier, I learned the value of academic success skills by nearly flunking my first-semester freshman chemistry course in college. Recall that this setback caused me to question my academic ability, and I was not sure I could succeed in college. I soon realized, however, that my academic performance was limited by poorly developed academic success skills. I developed my skills and succeeded. You, too, can boost your academic performance by developing your academic success skills.

Before we delve into our discussion, please understand that many college freshmen quickly discover that academic success skills used in high school often are inadequate for college.

# Chapter 13: Academic Success Best-Practices

Successful students are intentional about their education, and they employ best-practices that contribute to learning. A simple list of best-practices is shown below:

1. Attend class and sit near the front.

2. Ask questions.

3. Avoid distractions.

4. Set goals for your education.

5. In your planner, record test dates and deadlines for your assignments.

Additional best-practices are discussed in greater detail below.

# Note-Taking

Note-taking is an important academic success skill because your notes often serve as a significant source of information as you study and prepare for tests. The better your notes, the greater your opportunity to succeed. Your notes contain your own questions, comments, and reflections, as well as material captured from lectures, reading assignments, and other sources. Successful students possess highly developed note-taking skills.

I have heard several students say, "My teacher is so unorganized," or, "My teacher goes too fast." Although those statements may be true, successful students adapt to their teachers' styles. Some teachers are highly organized, and some are not. Some teachers provide handouts for lectures, and some do not. If your teacher does provide handouts, review them before class and take additional notes during class.

Some teachers move quickly through course material, and you must keep up. Develop your own abbreviations and shorthand system to help you capture information quickly. Consider taping lectures so that you can replay the lecture as you review your notes (be sure to get approval from your teacher before recording lectures).

Successful students find a note-taking method that works for them. A simple outlining process may meet your needs. Additionally, both the Cornell note-taking method and mind-mapping are excellent techniques for capturing, organizing, and reviewing your notes from lectures and reading assignments.

The Cornell method was developed by Dr. Walter Pauk at Cornell University (Pauk, 1962). To use the Cornell method, divide your note paper into three sections by drawing a vertical line two or three inches from the left edge and by drawing a horizontal line two or three inches from the bottom of the page (figure 1).

Capture your notes in the main section. Highlight main points and key words in the left-hand column. Write questions in the left-hand column, as well. Use the bottom section to summarize your notes after each class. Review this summary before the next class to refresh your memory and provide continuity for new material. (Refer to Pauk (2001) for a more in-depth discussion of the Cornell note-taking method.)

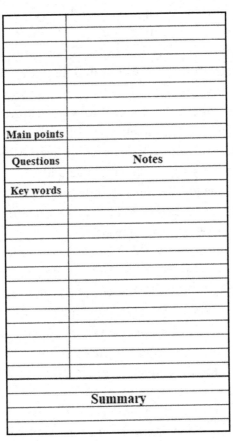

Figure 1. Cornell note-taking method.

Mind maps are effective for visually summarizing and organizing material from class lectures and reading assignments. You can use mind-mapping to capture notes during class, or you may find it more effective to build your mind map as you review and summarize your notes *after* class. Mind maps also are effective for brainstorming and planning your class projects, presentations, and writing assignments.

Mind-mapping offers advantages by providing a visual representation of relationships and varying levels of detail. The center of a mind map contains the main idea, and subpoints are added by creating branches. Additional details can be added by extending branches. Figure 2 shows a simple mind map depicting the uses of mind maps described in this section.

Mind-mapping can be accomplished with only a pencil and a piece of paper. Utilizing different colors and including images, however, improves your mind map. Mind-mapping software and apps are readily available and allow you to add colors and images. Search "mind-mapping for students" online to see more examples of mind maps and to discover mind-mapping technology options.

You may not be able to capture everything your teacher says in class, regardless of the note-taking technique you use. Listen carefully for the main points, important terms, and examples. How do you know what's important? Your teacher likely (but not always) will spend more time on more-important topics and less time on less-important topics. Material found in assigned readings and discussed in class is important.

Listen for clues from your teacher to help you identify important information. When I wanted to emphasize a particularly important point, I used to tell my students, "This material

Figure 2. Example of uses for mind maps.

will be on the test." Not all clues are that obvious, but teachers often give insight into important class material that is likely to show up on tests. Listen for phrases such as "The important point is," or, "Be sure you understand ..." Highlight that important information in your notes.

Keep in mind that all material discussed in class is of some importance, or it would not have been presented. Pay attention to the clues just mentioned but avoid trying to guess what your tests will cover. Adequate test preparation (see below) requires a thorough review of all lecture material, readings, and other assigned materials.

Set aside time each day to review and rewrite notes taken that day. Write legibly, and consider writing on only one side of a page to avoid ink bleed-through. Write out your abbreviations and shorthand while they are fresh in your mind. Doing so minimizes the frustrating "What the heck did I mean by this?" question that could show up later.

As you rewrite your notes, be sure to highlight important information and write a short, reflective summary of each lecture. Make a list of missing or confusing information and follow up by asking questions during the next class. Consider using different colors for your questions and comments.

## Read for Understanding

Reading for understanding might seem obvious, but countless students have told me, "I read the chapter, but I didn't understand it." Successful students recognize that academic reading differs from casual reading, such as skimming an online article or enjoying a favorite book.

Start reading by getting the "big picture." Read the introduction and conclusion, and review heading and subheading titles. Utilize the Cornell method, mind maps, and/or outlines to capture and organize the information you read. Highlight important information, and create summaries. Jot down initial questions that come to mind.

Keep in mind that you don't have to read an entire assignment in a single marathon reading session. Break up your readings into logical sections and take a break between sections. Assess your understanding as you read by summarizing or paraphrasing key points and concepts. If you don't understand the material, read it again. If you still don't understand, prepare specific questions, then ask your teacher for clarification.

In addition to the text, be sure you understand the key points of figures and tables. Be able to answer questions specifically about the figures and tables themselves, and also understand the underlying concepts. If the concept is important enough to justify a table or figure, the concept is worthy of your understanding.

Pay special attention to sections in the assigned readings that align directly with material discussed in class. You can ask your teacher if you are responsible for learning everything in your reading assignments or just the material that was covered in class. College students should expect to be responsible for learning all material in reading assignments, whether or not it was covered in class.

## Preparing For and Taking Tests

Ideally, test scores indicate how well you understand your course material. In reality, test scores also indicate how well you prepare for and take tests. As a successful student, maximize your potential score by effectively preparing for and taking tests. Further, set a goal to learn the material not only for the test but so you can also apply the material in subsequent classes and ultimately solve problems and make positive contributions beyond school.

Successful students understand that test preparation is an ongoing process, rather than a last-minute cram session. Review your lecture notes daily. Spend an hour or so on each class, reviewing lecture notes, outlines of reading assignments, and small group discussions each week. Doing so allows you to keep up with your course material and can make test preparation less daunting. Starting about a week before your test, dedicate as much time as needed to learn the material. Allow at least another two or three hours of studying during the week of the test, and assess your progress based on the learning you accomplish, rather than on the time you spend studying.

Constructing your own test questions is an effective test-preparation technique. Set aside your notes and attempt to answer your own questions, as though you were taking an actual test. Work through old tests if your teacher allows, and ask your teacher to review your answers.

Preparing for a comprehensive final exam requires greater time and effort, due to the volume of material to be reviewed. Keep in mind that a final exam allows your teacher to test you over material that was not included on earlier exams, so be sure to study material that was not on the earlier exams. Final exams also allow your teacher to reemphasize important concepts from earlier exams, so be sure to study material that was included on earlier exams. (Yes, I am advising you to study all the material.)

Having gone through the entire semester, you now have a "big picture" perspective of the course material. This perspective can help you fill in gaps in your learning and allow you to tie concepts together. You likely now better understand the material you missed on the earlier exams.

I purposefully gave comprehensive final exams to encourage (force) my students to go back through all the course material, and my approach proved effective. Students commonly performed better on material on the final exam than they did on the same material on earlier exams.

Begin preparing for a final exam by reviewing your course objectives, which should be listed in your course syllabus. The objectives of the course will very likely be tested on the final exam. Review your previous exams and practice exams from the course. Be sure you can answer all questions on previous exams.

Preparing for your exams to the best of your ability is an important first step. Knowing how to take tests also is important. If you struggle with taking tests, don't worry; you can develop your test-taking skills.

Arrive early on the test day and get settled into your seat. Avoid congregating with students who are nervous or who are trying to cram in last-second details. Their anxiety can be contagious, and their jabbering may create confusion in your mind. Relax and envision yourself doing well.

Listen for instructions from your teacher as the test is handed out. When you get your test, read through it thoroughly to be sure you understand all the questions. Ask your teacher for clarification as needed. Follow directions as you work through the test. For example, if a question asks you to list three factors that influence photosynthesis, list three factors, not one, two, or six. If a question asks for your opinion, provide your opinion rather than only providing facts. Answer the easiest questions first to maximize your points and build confidence.

Be mindful of time as you move to more difficult questions. Avoid spending so much time on a question or two that you are unable to work on every problem. Jot down what you do know before you leave a difficult question, and come back to it later. Be sure to write legibly. I constantly had to remind my students, "If I can't read it, it's wrong."

Read multiple-choice questions and potential answers carefully. Subtle differences often separate the correct (or best) answer from the others. Eliminate choices that you believe fail to answer the question. Doing so increases your odds of selecting the best answer if you must guess.

Recognize that multiple choice questions involving calculations often include common miscalculations as potential answers. Don't be lulled into a false sense of security by the fact that your calculated answer is a choice. Double-check your calculations as time allows.

Read short-answer or essay test questions carefully and understand what is being asked. Jot down the ideas that come to mind so you don't forget them. As you answer the questions, utilize your critical thinking skills and provide supporting evidence from your lectures and reading assignments.

Be sure that your answer specifically addresses the question, regardless of the test format. My students occasionally put down correct statements but lost points because the statements did not answer the question. I responded to their protests with the metaphor of visiting a doctor for the treatment of a sprained ankle only to have the doctor put your arm in a sling. Putting your arm in a sling may be the correct action in some circumstances, but doing so in this case will not help your sprained ankle. Similarly, an otherwise correct statement may not be a correct answer on a test if the statement does not address the question.

Unless you are specifically penalized for wrong answers, put down relevant information, and perhaps you will earn partial credit for questions on which you are unsure of the answer. Notice that I said "perhaps." Once, I was unsure how to solve a problem on a test. I asked my professor if I could receive partial credit by describing the steps I would use to the solve the problem, even if I did not actually solve the problem. He said, "Sure."

I wrote down everything I could think of that would solve the problem. When I got the test back, I had received a zero on that question. I reminded the professor that he had told me I could earn partial credit by describing how to solve the problem, even if I didn't actually solve the problem. He replied, "Yes, I remember. But everything you wrote down is wrong!"

My point: Prepare extensively for your exams, and don't rely on guessing.

Let's now discuss managing test anxiety. Please understand that a little test anxiety is not uncommon and that it can, in fact, be motivating. Minimize potential anxiety by envisioning yourself performing well, and utilize the best-practices described in this chapter to prepare for your tests.

If anxiety is affecting your productivity, however, or if you are concerned about the level of your anxiety, visit the academic success center at your school or speak to your advisor. The professionals at your school can help you manage your test anxiety.

Students sometimes put undue stress on themselves by comparing themselves to others. Remember our definition of academic success: Performing at the level of *your* academic ability. You learned earlier that you are accountable only for your abilities and that you should not compare yourself to others.

What if you flunk a test or an entire course? In my physical chemistry course, I got a 36 on the first test. I didn't give up, however, and by end of the semester, I had increased my grade to an A. Remember how I bombed my first freshman chemistry course? I took the course again and did well. My point is that even if you fail a test or have to repeat a course, you can generally bounce back and move on.

If you do flunk a test, review your answers with your teacher and determine a plan for succeeding in the future. I understand that talking to your teacher about your failed test can be embarrassing. I also understand that your teacher already knows your score and wants to help you figure out what you missed. Remember that your goal is to learn the material so that you can apply it in subsequent courses and in the real world beyond school. Plus, you don't want to miss the material again if it shows up on the final exam.

In addition to reviewing the test you struggled with, reflect on your preparation process. Did you truly prepare? Did you attend classes and take notes effectively? Did you discuss your questions with your teacher after each class, or did you wait until the morning of the test?

Keep my experiences in mind, prepare adequately for your exams, and envision yourself succeeding. If you experience anxiety, utilize the resources at your school. Stay focused, and soon you will be a test-taking pro.

## Conquer Procrastination

Procrastination is the continual avoidance of starting or completing something that must be completed, and procrastination can be detrimental to academic performance. Assignments may be completed poorly at the last minute and/or turned in late, if at all. Important meetings, such as meeting with a tutor, can be delayed and rendered less effective.

If you struggle to start and finish the important things you need to do, make a plan to conquer procrastination. The first step is recognizing when you procrastinate. Do you repeatedly postpone tasks? Are you easily distracted while working on a task? If so, you likely are procrastinating.

Determining *why* you procrastinate is the next step. Remember that you must define a problem and its underlying cause before you can solve it. The following are a few reasons for procrastinating:

1. You feel overwhelmed by all you must do, and you don't know where to start.

2. You don't know how to start.

3. You don't know how to do what you need to do.

4. You don't know what's expected.

5. You want to avoid failure, conflict, and unpleasant situations.

In "Focus on Your Priorities," we discussed the need to complete your most important task first. Starting a task instead of repeatedly putting it off is a priority for conquering procrastination, and the following solutions will help you get started.

When faced with an overwhelming number of tasks, identify a couple of the easiest tasks, then complete them first. Doing so allows you to get started and provides a sense of accomplishment. Use your momentum to tackle the remaining tasks in priority order.

If you don't know how to start a project, refer to the term paper example in our earlier discussion on "Planning and Completing Projects." Break down your project into manageable steps and enter deadlines for each step into your calendar. Working on the individual steps can help you conquer procrastination because you know where to start, and you also have a defined path to completion. Share your steps and deadlines with your mentor and ask him to periodically check on your progress.

If you struggle to start a writing project, recognize that your first draft does not have to be perfect. I often start writing knowing that the first draft will never survive to the final version. Begin your next writing project by jotting down a few quick thoughts to kick-start the process. You should then find it easier to continue working on your draft.

Consider a student who delays working on a homework assignment because he does not understand how to do it. The solution can be as simple as visiting his teacher or tutor to learn how to do the assignment. Next, consider a student who does not start a lab report because he does not know what is expected to be included in the report. The solution is simple: Clarify the expectations with the teacher.

If you procrastinate when faced with something unpleasant, understand that you have two choices: You can repeatedly postpone the task or activity (but doing so only contributes to your stress level), or you can simply complete the task and move on. I once faced a very daunting task, and my mentor quickly figured out that I was procrastinating. She said sternly, "Cary, you are living in fantasyland. You know what needs to be done, but you are just hoping the problem will magically go away. Well, it won't magically go away. Now, take care of it, and move on."

That conversation taught me to simply muster up enough activation energy to attack daunting tasks sooner rather than later.

As discussed previously in "Maintain a Positive Attitude," the outcome probably won't be as bad as you envision. And if it is bad, dealing with it sooner is preferable. Left unresolved, the situation rarely magically goes away, but it might worsen.

If you are prone to procrastination, put into action the recommendations above. Discuss your procrastination tendency with your mentor and ask him to keep you accountable for following through. (Suggestion: Talk to your mentor now, rather than postponing the conversation until next week.)

## Stay on Track

Loss of motivation is a common issue faced by most of us at one time or another. The commitment to study or work, however, regardless of feelings or circumstances, is critical to your success in the classroom, in your career, and in life in general. Let's end our discussion of academic success best-practices with some practical tips to help you stay on track, even when you don't feel motivated:

1.  Set a specific time to study every day.

2.  Find a quiet, distraction-free place to study. Avoiding distractions is more effective than trying to ignore them. Be sure to turn off your cell phone and social media/messaging apps.

3.  Break 90- or 120-minute study sessions into three or four 30-minute blocks. Tailor the sessions to optimize your study time. Remember to assess your progress based on learning rather than on the amount of time you study.

4.  Take a 5- or 10-minute break between blocks.

5.  Build in goals for each study session. Your goals should be challenging, but realistic.

6.  Reward yourself by doing something you enjoy after each study session.

7.  Use the best-practices described above.

8.  Use the resources described below.

9.  Stick with this plan, even when you don't feel like it.

Key points from chapter 13:

1.  Actively engage in your education.

2.  Go to class.

3.  Find a note-taking system that works for you.

4.  Adapt to your teachers' presentation style.

5.  Assess reading progress in terms of understanding, rather than time spent reading.

6.  Review your course material weekly to make studying for tests more efficient.

7.  Write answers legibly, and specifically answer the questions.

8.  Envision yourself doing well on exams.

9.  Be aware of procrastination and conquer it quickly.

10. Set up a study schedule and stick to it, even when you don't feel motivated.

# References

Pauk, W. 1962. *How to Study in College*. Boston: Houghton Mifflin Harcourt.

Pauk, W. 2001. *How to Study in College*. Boston: Houghton Mifflin Harcourt.

# Chapter 14: Academic Success Resources

Educational institutions are committed to your success, and they provide resources to help you succeed. Successful students familiarize themselves with the academic success resources available to them and take full advantage of the resources. Access to many academic success resources is included in your tuition and fees, so you can likely utilize them without additional cost.

In the pages that follow, you will discover resources organized into "people," "places," and "things." These resources are particularly important for academic success and career readiness. Not all high schools and universities, however, will have the resources described here. High school students should familiarize themselves with these resources and ask about availability of these resources when selecting a university to attend.

# People

The faculty and staff at your school are your greatest resources. As previously discussed, successful students attend class, take notes, and ask questions. Successful students also connect with their teachers beyond the classroom. Your teacher likely has office hours set aside to help you, and many teachers allow students to drop in as needed. Your teacher's contact information and office-hours policy should be available on your course syllabus. If not, ask.

Meeting with your teacher during office hours allows you to ask for clarification of class material and assistance on assignments. You certainly should ask for help if you need help, and you also should be prepared when you visit your teacher. Sometimes, it's easier to ask for help than to try and find a solution on your own. It's important, however, that you make a real attempt to solve your problem or understand the material before you seek help. Review your notes and other resources, and you may find the information you need.

Before you visit your teacher, prepare specific questions to ask. Start out with what you *do* know, rather than what you *don't* know. For example, you might tell your teacher, "I read chapter three, but I still don't understand ...," or, "I worked on my assignment, but I am not sure how to ..."

Preparing for your meeting with your teacher has two benefits. First, you demonstrate commitment to your education, and this commitment contributes to a solid reputation with your teachers, who may write reference letters for you. Second, you can ask more informed questions, which will make your time with your teacher more efficient.

College students also can inquire about opportunities to participate in their faculty's research or other scholarly activities.

This participation deepens your understanding and allows you to build a network of faculty who can recommend you for scholarships, awards, internships, and jobs. (We will discuss undergraduate research and other experiential education opportunities in greater detail later is this chapter.)

Similarly, check in regularly with your academic advisor. An effective academic advisor is an excellent source of information regarding course selection and academic best-practices. Your advisor can connect you with additional campus resources. Further, your advisor can alert you to opportunities for scholarships and awards.

Make a deliberate effort to meet your advisor as soon as the school year starts; if possible, connecting the summer before is preferable. Obtain contact information, and determine the preferred mode of communication, usually through your school's e-mail system. When it's time to schedule classes, meet with your advisor as early as possible. Doing so increases the likelihood that you can get into the classes you want at your preferred times. Having said that, realize that incoming freshmen are usually the last to register for classes. Don't be surprised if scheduling your classes is challenging for the first semester or two.

Prepare for your advising meeting by developing a tentative schedule based on the degree-plan worksheet your advisor provides at the beginning of the year. Make your advisor aware of any transfer credits you have or that you plan to obtain. Try to plan your schedule out from two to three semesters in advance and watch for courses that are offered infrequently. For example, the course you need to qualify for graduation in the spring semester of 2019 might be offered only during even years. Therefore, you need to take it during the spring semester of 2018. You might delay your graduation if you are not aware of course rotations. The good news is that your advisor knows this information, and working closely with your advisor increases your likelihood of a timely graduation. Keep in mind, though, that *you* are ultimately responsible for complying with all the requirements for your graduation.

Tutors are valuable academic success resources. Tutors work one-on-one with you to help you understand your course material. An effective tutor will not give you the answer but will instead help you understand and apply course concepts so you can construct your own answers and complete assignments on your own.

Many universities provide free tutoring services, and tutoring information and resources are available at your campus academic success center (see below). Also, you can ask your teachers about the tutoring resources available for their classes. Once you identify tutors for each of your classes, commit to meeting with those tutors throughout the semester.

Additionally, academic coaches help you develop your academic success skills, set goals, and successfully navigate through hindrances to your success. Academic coaches are especially valuable to college freshmen. Your coach can identify areas for improvement that you may not see and connect you with resources you may not know you need. Your coach can hold you accountable for reaching your academic and life goals. Finally, your academic coach is a powerful connection to your school, and this connection is essential for students in general and for incoming college freshmen in particular.

Determine whether your school offers academic coaches. If so, enroll in coaching, and take full advantage of this excellent resource.

# Places

Many universities have an academic success center where trained staff are available to help you succeed in your education. You also can find a list of approved tutors, academic coaches, and courses supported with supplemental instruction (see below). Other resources include advice for preparing for and taking tests, minimizing test anxiety, and overcoming procrastination.

The resources at the academic success center can empower you to perform at the level of your true academic potential. Prioritize visiting your success center and avail yourself of the resources.

Similarly, if your school has a writing center, take full advantage of its services. Employers constantly report a lack of effective written and oral communication skills in recent graduates, and staff at the writing center can teach you how to communicate effectively.

Writing center staff can coach you on topics such as developing and organizing your ideas, as well as constructing sentences and paragraphs. The staff can review the rules of grammar with you and help you develop your editorial skills. The staff also can advise you on creating compelling arguments (remember your critical-thinking skills?) and citing resources. Most writing centers offer advice on creating effective oral and poster presentations, and can equip you to develop impactful cover letters and resumes.

Expect the staff at the writing center to teach you how to improve your communication skills, rather than editing your materials for you. Therefore, you are wise to seek input *throughout the development* of your project, rather than waiting to get input on a paper that's due in the morning.

I've seen numerous students, at all ability levels, benefit from the services offered by the academic success center and/or writing center. One of my students significantly increased her test preparation skills and overall confidence by participating in a program offered through the academic success center. Another one of my students enhanced her writing skills through the mentoring she received, and her improved skills led to a higher score in one of my courses. These centers can improve your performance, as well.

As discussed earlier, the career center provides several valuable services to every student from incoming freshmen to graduating seniors and graduate students. Locate the career center on your campus and get on the mailing list. Most career centers offer career counseling services and will administer assessments to help you identify your strengths. Career counselors will interpret your results and discuss academic majors and careers that align with your strengths.

Most university career centers host career fairs, to which they invite potential employers. These fairs allow you to meet with representatives from companies, government agencies, and nonprofits. Some fairs are discipline-specific (i.e., an engineering career fair), and others are open to all majors. Further, recruiters from graduate programs may attend career fairs or stand-alone graduate school fairs.

I strongly recommend that you attend career fairs on your campus, even if you are a first-semester freshman. Doing so is a great networking opportunity and allows you to discuss the most sought-after skills and experiences of employers. You can use this information to guide your selection of elective courses and experiential education opportunities. You can inquire about the availability of internships as well.

Career center staff can review your resume and cover letters and provide valuable input. You can bolster your job-search skills by attending workshops. Further, you can hone your interview skills by participating in mock interviews, in which career center staff and corporate recruiters "interview" you. You will receive constructive feedback on your interview skills, as well as tips for contacting and following up with potential employers. Participate in as many mock interviews as needed so that you are well-prepared for your actual interviews.

I required students in my senior seminar to participate in mock interviews. One of their interviews was recorded, and most students were amazed to see themselves fumbling the answers to simple questions. After a few rounds of mock interviews, however, most students significantly improved their interview skills. Take advantage of this opportunity to work the kinks out of your interview skills.

In addition to your skills, your whole-body health and wellness influences your academic success. Campus health-and-wellness centers provide access to medical professionals who can assess and treat illnesses. Counseling services may also be offered to help students cope with homesickness and other struggles commonly experienced by students. Student health service fees are often included in the typical tuition and fees charged to students, but additional fees-for-service may be charged, as well. Check with your campus health-and-wellness center for specific information on available services and costs.

Cultural centers are academic success resources that connect faculty, staff, and students with similar cultural identity and interests, and they also provide support services. Cultural centers provide opportunities to learn about different cultures through resources and events. Cultural centers also provide excellent opportunities to make connections with the campus and local community. These connections foster a sense of belonging that contributes to your academic success.

Below is a list of other useful places to familiarize yourself with:

1. Students with children can take advantage of services offered by an on-campus childcare center. Expect to be put on a waiting list and expect to pay for this service.

2. Navigating the financial aspects of a college education can be daunting, and the staff at the financial aid office can assist you in obtaining and accessing any financial aid for which you qualify.

3. High-achieving students should review the admission and graduation requirements for the honors college. Due to its selectivity, students in the honors college enjoy smaller classes, many of which are taught by the best faculty on campus. Honors students must complete a creative, scholarly project. Jump on the opportunity to be an honors student!

4. The office staff of student legal services provides legal advice and can review contracts for students.

5. Finally, the campus recreation center provides many opportunities for intramural sports, aerobics, and weight training. Students usually can borrow equipment for camping, canoeing, and other outdoor activities.

# Things

Supplemental instruction (SI) was developed Dr. Deanna C. Martin at the University of Missouri–Kansas City (Burmeister, 1996). The program provides review sessions for difficult courses. The sessions are usually led by a student who excelled in the course in an earlier semester. The peer leader attends class during the current semester and leads a group discussion. Students who attend the session learn not only from the peer leader but also from classmates.

You can find a list of courses supported by SI at the campus academic center. Information should also be available on your course syllabus. If you enroll in a course that has an SI component, take advantage of this no-additional-cost resource.

Study groups provide additional collaborative learning opportunities. Participants help each other fill in gaps in learning and share their insight. Study groups can develop a pool of practice test questions and can work together to develop the correct answers.

Participants can further deepen their understanding by teaching each other. Teaching course material will reveal knowledge gaps that merely discussing the material may not. I learned this truth when I began my teaching career. Preparing lectures was humbling because I quickly learned that I did not know as much as I thought I did. Allot time during your study group meetings for each student to teach.

Finally, be sure to set an agenda and stick to it. Doing so keeps the focus on academics and minimizes mission-drift.

Many universities offer learning communities for freshmen. These communities place students into small groups based on residence hall, academic major, or themes (e.g., food security, entrepreneurship, leadership, gender issues, etc.).

Students in learning communities attend classes together, and these classes may be smaller than typical classes. Further, these classes are typically taught by the best teachers on campus.

Students in learning communities also meet for discussions beyond class. Learning communities can help you transition to college and improve your academic performance by quickly connecting you to excellent faculty and fellow students. Research the learning community opportunities available to you, and take advantage of them.

College students benefit significantly from participating in high-impact practices, such as learning communities. Additional, high-impact practices include service learning, undergraduate research, internships/field experience, study abroad, and a culminating experience, such as a senior capstone course (NSSE, 2015). High-impact practices foster learning beyond the classroom and increase engagement with faculty and fellow students (NSSE, 2015). Further, these experience-based activities are well known to cultivate success skills valued by employers.

Learning communities were discussed earlier, and the other practices are described below. Service learning courses connect students with projects in the community. The students work closely with community stakeholders to develop solutions to real-world issues faced by the communities. Students gain practical experience applying the concepts learned in the classroom. The interaction with stakeholders provides the opportunity to develop problem-solving, communication, and teamwork skills.

Undergraduate research is a high-impact practice that allows students to participate in research activities with university faculty. There are several tangible benefits to conducting undergraduate research. Students develop skills in critical thinking and problem-solving, teamwork, and communication.

Students researchers gain in-depth knowledge of the latest scientific principles and gain advanced analytical skills in their discipline through active involvement in research. These students also gain valuable networking and mentoring benefits by working closely with faculty and other researchers. Some students leverage research even further by developing their own publications or presentations at professional meetings.

Internships give students the opportunity to work for a company, nonprofit, or government agency and to get experience beyond the classroom. Interns see the application of course material and develop a deeper understanding of their discipline. Interns also develop an appreciation for workplace expectations of professionalism.

Many universities require students to complete an internship. I strongly encourage you to participate in an internship, even if it is not required. Experience provided through internships is highly valued by potential employers, and interns may receive a permanent job offer.

Leverage your internship by demonstrating that you would be a productive full-time employee. Approach your internship as you would a full-time job. Understand your job responsibilities and how your performance will be evaluated, and develop goals accordingly. Prioritize your time to achieve your goals and realize that you will be evaluated primarily on the outcomes you produce, rather than on the goals you set. And, of course, be professional in every aspect of your internship.

Study-abroad programs allow students to take courses or work in internships in foreign countries. These international programs provide exceptional opportunities to develop a greater awareness of global issues, gain firsthand experience with another culture, and develop cross-cultural skills.

On a personal level, students who engage in study-abroad programs experience tremendous personal growth while seeing the world. Lifelong friendships often are begun, and foreign language skills are honed in the immersive experience.

Don't be intimidated by the high costs of international travel. Most students who study abroad need some financial support. Be creative, and you likely can raise the money you need. I have seen students embark on fund-raising activities for a year before traveling. These activities range from parking cars at university sporting events to sending request letters to family and friends. Scholarships for students who study abroad often are available as well.

Maximize your study abroad experience by capturing your activities and daily reflections in a journal. Ask your teacher if you can post a blog on your school's website. Finally, be sure to take lots of pictures.

A capstone course is a high-impact practice often referred to as a "culminating" experience that students take during their final year in college. The capstone course focuses on critical thinking and problem-solving, and requires students to synthesize and apply their knowledge and experiences to real-world issues.

These high-impact practices, by definition, contribute to academic success. Talk to your teachers, advisor, and career center to learn about these and other high-impact, experiential learning opportunities.

Let's end our discussion of academic success resources by discussing student portfolios. A student portfolio contains a collection of your school work and other educational accomplishments. Portfolios can show academic goals and progress, evidence of your accomplishments, and a demonstration of your skills. You can tailor your portfolio based on a purpose, such as applying for college, scholarships, or jobs by producing your portfolio to showcase your accomplishments aligned with selection criteria. Sharing your portfolio with admission personnel, awards committees, and potential employers lends tremendous power to your application.

I learned first-hand the value of portfolios during a job interview. My interviewer emphasized the requirement of writing research publications to be successful in his department. He asked about my writing experience. I handed him a portfolio of my recent research publications. A few days later I was offered the job.

You can develop a simple portfolio for each of your classes. Doing so will help you organize your assignments, exams, writing assignments, and projects. A more impactful portfolio, however, contains records of your accomplishments and showcases your best work from all your classes and academic endeavors. For example, you can include copies of your best writing assignments and tests, scholarship and award letters, and projects.

Your portfolio also should include your reflection on your educational goals, skills development, and experiences. For example, you may reflect on your improved writing skills by discussing input you received from your teachers and the resultant changes you made. Include a copy of your latest and greatest writing assignment to demonstrate your improved writing skills.

Your portfolio is an excellent system that allows you to close the loop on your experiential education endeavors. For example, add to your portfolio your reflections from your study-abroad experience. Include final projects from internships and service learning projects. Describe the research skills and experience you developed from your undergraduate research project. Include any publications, posters, or other intellectual property you create.

If you have not developed a student portfolio, I strongly encourage you to do so. Digital portfolios are popular, and many online resources are available to help you develop and maintain your portfolio. Search "digital portfolios" online to learn more.

Key points from chapter 14:

1. Obtain a preferred contact method for teachers, advisors, and tutors.

2. Meet with teachers, advisors, and tutors as needed, and thoroughly prepare for the meetings.

3. Work with an academic coach.

4. Locate the academic success center, writing center, and career center on your campus, and sign up for their mailing lists.

5. Participate in every supplemental instruction opportunity available.

6. Join a learning community.

7. Engage in high-impact practices such as internships and study abroad.

8. Create and maintain a portfolio showcasing your academic goals, progress, and accomplishments.

# References

Burmeister, S. "Supplemental Instruction: An Interview with Deanna Martin." *Journal of Developmental Education* 20, no. 1 (1996): 22–26.

National Survey of Student Engagement. 2015. "Engagement Indicators & High-Impact Practices." Retrieved July 29, 2017, from Indiana University School of Education: http://nsse.indiana.edu/pdf/EIs_and_HIPs_2015.pdf.

# Summary and Implementation

What if the fastest runner is not in the race? Perhaps the fastest runner does not know she has the talent to earn a gold medal. Perhaps she simply does not believe she can win. Perhaps *you* are the fastest runner. Perhaps you will make a life-saving medical breakthrough. Perhaps you will create a business that will impact millions of lives. Perhaps you will be the greatest author, architect, or artist of your generation.

As you develop a better understanding of your skills and abilities, you will very likely discover that you are capable of achieving more than you currently think. Believing you can achieve success is foundational to achieving success.

Clarifying your definition of success is also foundational to achieving success. But doing so may seem paradoxical at this point in your life because you may not know what you want to achieve. The key is willingness to move forward, believing you will succeed—even though you may not know what you will achieve.

You may be surprised to know that I did not initially plan to be a professor or to start my own student-centered business. In fact, I did not plan to get a PhD when I started college. I knew that I wanted to go as far as I could in my education, but earning a PhD seemed far beyond my ability (especially during my first semester in college). When I decided to get a PhD, I planned to become an environmental consultant. I didn't discover my inclination to teach and mentor students until I started my first university position.

I gained greater clarity of my strengths, professional passion, and abilities as I progressed in my education and career. The increased clarity allowed me to continually refine my view of what I wanted to, and was able to, achieve. You, too, should see your strengths, professional passion, and abilities more clearly as you progress in life. Coupling this clarity with ever-developing skills and knowledge will empower you to set and achieve big, impactful goals.

Don't limit your future based on your current skills and abilities. Empower your future by daring to believe in what you will become!

## Learning Outcomes Revisited

Let's review our learning outcomes and summarize key points for developing your success skills. Our first learning outcome is constructing realistic expectations for achieving success. Although you may not know exactly what you will encounter on your journey to success, through this book you have discovered the need to work hard and work smart. You understand now that intelligence is not enough and that your skills must increase each time you advance in your education and career.

You have also discovered that successful people must usually overcome a few obstacles or setbacks before achieving success. Remember that I had to get a D in college before I earned a PhD. Learn from your setbacks and move past them. Achieving success requires a fierce commitment.

Our next learning outcome is developing self-awareness. You must understand, develop, and utilize your strengths to achieve success. Remember that creating opportunities to use your strengths creates opportunities for you.

Reflection is essential for self-awareness. Reflect on your successes and setbacks, and then strive to figure out what is working and what is not. Maximize the factors that contribute to your success, and minimize or eliminate factors that hold you back.

Reflection helps you identify when you are stressed and need a break. Gauge your success by your progress—not merely by the time spent on a task. If you are working hard but not making progress, take a break and/or get help to get back on track. Reflection also helps ensure that you continually do the right things for the right reasons.

Our next learning outcome is building a future-oriented attitude. Remember that you are preparing to address problems and work in careers that may not exist today. As discussed above, you may not know what the future holds, but you can be ready for the opportunities that will come your way by investing in activities today that build skills for future success.

Your future-oriented attitude empowers you to look for and step up to challenges. Your future-oriented attitude allows you to see obstacles and setbacks as temporary, and gives you the confidence to continually move forward. Your future-oriented attitude keeps you engaged in learning throughout your lifetime.

Our final learning outcome is improving your academic success skills, leadership skills, and soft skills. Successful people strive to perform at the level of their ability, and doing so requires the development and utilization of success skills.

Identify and eliminate gaps as you develop your skills. Gaps can exist between your current practices and best-practices, between planning and action, and between action and impact.

Assess your current skills against the information provided in this book. For example, are your test-preparation skills at the level described in this book? Do you communicate clearly? Have you already or are you planning to participate in internships in college?

Having just finished the book, I don't expect that all your skills are fully developed. You have what you need, however, to develop a plan for improving your skills by utilizing the exercises provided. Begin developing a plan if you have not done so. Use the examples, exercises, and templates in this book to solidify your plan.

Finally, assess your progress as you implement your plan. Reflect on whether your skills are improving. Are you meeting deadlines and following through on all your commitments? Are you a more successful student or employee than you were a year ago? Have your leadership skills improved in the last few months? Refine your plan as needed to continually make progress.

Learn from others as you develop your success skills. Seek help when you need it and respond appropriately to constructive criticism. Doing so fosters continual improvement and contributes to long-term success.

Please understand that improving your success skills is a *process* and know that you don't have to improve all your skills at once. Don't expect perfection but strive for improvement.

# A Final Word of Encouragement

This book is an excellent example of what can be accomplished if you take a risk, set a big goal, and put forth real effort. I was not sure I could write something that young people would want to read. Because the goal of writing the book was anchored to my values, however, I determined that I would put my best effort into writing this book. The fact that you are reading it is testimony that values-aligned goals can be accomplished. (And the fact that you are reading the second edition demonstrates the importance of reflection and the relentless pursuit of improvement.)

If you believe in yourself, remain fiercely committed to your goals, and put forth your best effort, you will be limited only by your imagination. My expectation is that you will do what I have done: Determine what you truly value in life, set big goals aligned with these values, and make them happen. You will be glad you did. If you don't reach all your goals, at least you will have the satisfaction of knowing that you gave your best effort.

Finally, understand that one can't truly succeed without serving others. Successful people look beyond themselves and seek to make a difference in the lives of others. Make a deliberate effort to invest in the lives of those in your sphere of influence. As your success skills improve, your influence will increase and so will the number of lives you can impact.

Thanks for reading my book. For additional resources and information on my personalized coaching program and online course, please visit my website (www.caryjgreen.com). You can also follow me on Twitter (@CaryJGreen). I invite you to send me your questions and comments (cary@caryjgreen.com). I look forward to hearing from you!

CPSIA information can be obtained
at www.ICGtesting.com
Printed in the USA
FSOW04n0050280917
39264FS